Y2K = 666?

© 1998 by N. W. Hutchings and Larry Spargimino. All rights reserved. No part of this book may be used or reproduced in any manner whatsoever without written permission of the publisher, except in the case of brief quotations in articles and reviews. For more information write: Hearthstone Publishing, Ltd., 500 Beacon Drive, Oklahoma City, OK 73127.

Printed in the United States of America

ISBN 1-57558-34-9
Cover design by Christi Killian

Y2K = 666?

Dr. N. W. Hutchings

&

Dr. Larry Spargimino

contents

A Word of Thanks 7
Introduction 9

PART I

one	How Did We Get Into This Mess? 19
two	What Others Say About the Problem 33
three	What Happens If It Happens? 49
four	The Y2K Problem and Bible Prophecy 63
five	Tightening the Noose: Y2K and Universal Bondage 79
six	Being Spiritually Prepared 97
seven	Preparing to Survive 113
eight	The Final Solution 123

PART II

the transcripts
    Y2K: Who? Why? When? Where? 141

appendix a
    Y2K and Signs in the Heavens 204

appendix b
    Y2K Update 209

a word of thanks
Dr. Larry Spargimino

This book, like any other writing project, is the culmination of years of general study and preparation, plus personal effort focused on this project itself. God has been wonderfully working in my life, first, by saving me through His grace and, secondly, by His providential arrangement of the affairs of my life. Ministry is a privilege. All praise and honor go to Him!

I also want to thank several individuals for their ministry to me so that I could be more effective in the ministry the Lord has given me.

First, I want to thank Dr. Noah W. Hutchings for the opportunity to serve with him at Southwest Radio Church, and also for the joy of being able to coauthor this book with him.

Also, many thanks to my dear friend and brother in Christ, Kenneth C. Hill, who has provided me with opportunities for service to our Lord through radio broadcasting and writing, and has provided direction and encouragement during a large part of my ministry.

Several individuals who are part of the Southwest Radio Church staff have been an invaluable help to me in completing my part of this book. Marvin McElvany for his tireless work in researching the Internet, a man of great patience, whom I have interrupted so many times with questions about my computer. Other staff members have played a unique role in this work as well: Christi Killian, Leah Flores, Ron King, Jerry Guiltner, and Dr. Bob Glaze.

And last, but certainly not least, I want to thank my wife Jennifer for her willingness to put up with my hours of being locked away in the study or office and her patience in tolerating my distracted stares as she realized, on so many occasions, that I really wasn't listening to what she was saying *because my mind was really on the writing of a book.*

introduction

Dr. N. W. Hutchings

In 1986 I wrote the introduction to a book which I coauthored titled *Computers and the Beast*. Following is a word-for-word repeat of that introduction:

> The prophet Daniel wrote of the extremity of the age that at "... the time of the end: many shall run to and fro, and knowledge shall be increased" (Dan. 12:4). In speaking again of the sequence of end-time events, the prophet said again, "... the end thereof shall be with a flood ..." (Dan. 9:26). The prophetic scope of the world economy at the time of Christ's return depicts a sudden rush of political, financial, and scientific changes that would literally shake the earth to prepare the way for the coming of the "man of sin," the Antichrist. The Word of God indicates quite plainly that the generation of mankind living at the end of the age could witness these dramatic events and know from observing these signs that the coming of the Lord from heaven was at hand, even at the door. "And when these things begin to come to pass, then look up, and lift up your heads; for your redemption draweth nigh" (Luke 21:28).
>
> Just as the radio, automobile, and airplane appeared almost simultaneously to push mankind into the industrial age, the splitting of the atom, television,

and the computer sprang upon the world scene within months of each other to further propel the world into the nuclear and space age.

Primitive computers were used in World War II to convert radar information to firing data for antiaircraft artillery and naval guns. The first commercial computer did not appear until 1947. But nothing since the creation of Adam has changed the life of man and the world economy in such a brief span as the computer has done. In just thirty years, every fact of modern life has been altered by the computer. If every computer in the world were to suddenly go dead, planes would not fly, trains would not run, traffic lights would not change, banks would have to close, space projects would be aborted, and all department stores and grocery stores would not be able to sell. Today, yes even today, the computer commands the working, buying, and selling of every individual, every business, and every governmental department. If the computers were suddenly silenced, the world would be thrown into instant chaos. Computer numbers and computer code marks are a sign that a checkless and cashless world financial order is coming soon. This will be a precise fulfillment of Revelation 13:16–17, "And he causeth all, both small and great, rich and poor, free and bond, to receive a mark in their right hand, or in their foreheads: And that no man might buy or sell, save he that had the mark, or the name of the beast, or the number of his name."

But no force or entity can produce a power greater than itself. Therefore, inasmuch as by God were all things created, nothing made by the Creator, or His creature—man—can be equal to or greater than the Creator. This is true of the fifth-generation computer, or even a fifty-generation computer. God will always be in control. In these last days when knowledge is increasing, man's inventions mean divine intervention. To illustrate this point, we refer to a UPI release, dateline Jerusalem, November 26, 1985:

"Israeli researchers using a computer say they have found encoded messages in the Bible, giving new support to the belief that the Book's every word is divinely inspired. The researchers said in the book of Esther they found a reference to the hanging of ten Nazi war criminals on October 16, 1946, and in the book of Deuteronomy the word 'holocaust' was hidden. There is no way to explain this information, said Dr. Moshe Katz, a Technion biomechanic who has a degree in biblical studies. 'This is a divine source.' The team has drawn no conclusions but if the initial findings hold up, Katz believes the implications could be profound. One of the biggest disputes in the Judeo-Christian tradition has been whether the Bible is literally inspired by God. In Christianity, the question represents a central difference between the theological fundamentalist and the liberal. The team's research suggests the Bible was inspired by God, word for word, letter for letter. Katz said he and Dr. Fred Weiner, a computer specialist in the Technion medical faculty, told the computer to skip letters as it scanned the Hebrew language Bible. Often words and messages leaped out of the text when the computer used only every 50th letter or 26th letter. One of the Hebrew names for God is Yahweh. When its Hebrew letters are translated into numbers, Yahweh becomes number 26. Number 50, Katz points out, is 7 times 7 plus 1. Seven is an important number in the Bible—there are seven days in the week of Creation. It is 50 days between Passover and Shavuot (Pentecost).... Katz said that by skipping letters the computer found 'Elohim,' another Hebrew name for God, hidden 147 times among the letters of the book of Genesis. He said the probability of it happening by chance was about one in two million. Computer programmer Dr. Eliyahu Rips, a Hebrew University mathematician, found the name of Aaron the high priest hidden among the letters of the first part of Leviticus 25 times. He said the probability of that happening was one in 500,000. Esther 9 is a story of how Queen Esther demanded the hanging of the ten sons of Haman who were enemies of the Jews. Hidden among the names of the sons were letters of the Hebrew date for 1946—the year the Nazis were hanged. According to newspaper reports at the time, Julius Streicher, one of the Nazis, shouted just before his hanging, 'Today is Purim 1946.' Purim is the Jewish holiday celebrating Esther's triumph. The date of the hanging of the Nazis, October 16, 1946, fell on the final day of judgment in the 'ten days of awe' between Rosh Hashana and Yom Kippur. In Deuteronomy 31, the Lord told Moses his descendants would forsake God and break his law. Verse 17 says, 'Then my anger will be kindled against them ... and I will devour them.' When the computer read every 50th letter in that section, the Hebrew word for 'holocaust' emerged. Many biblical scholars today believe the Bible was pieced together by a skilled editor using four ancient sources—the 'D,' 'P,' 'E,' and 'J' documents. 'There is no way that this hypothesis can stand,' Katz said, pointing out that many of the encoded words were drawn from passages that proponents of this hypothesis say were pieced together from more than one source. Under the team's theory, if even one letter is removed, all the results collapse."

No word of God in the Bible can be taken away, and no word added. Just as God used the god of the Philistine, Dagan, to prove His power and will, He is today using man's computer-god to prove that though heaven and earth may pass away, His Word will never pass away. And as we see these signs passing rapidly before our eyes, we pray with the apostle John, "Even so, come, Lord Jesus."

One reason I have repeated this same introduction that was written twelve years ago is to show that God's prophetic Word is always years ahead of the ultimate fulfillment. In 1977 I wrote a detailed paper on cloning and genetic engineering. In 1997 the world was amazed to hear about a sheep being cloned and to learn that over sixty percent of our food is now genetically engineered. In 1986 I wrote a paper on the adverse results of low frequency radio waves. In 1996 Dr. Nick Begich wrote a book, *Angels Don't Play This Haarp*. This book is about the building of three hundred and eight towers in Alaska to flood the world with low frequency radio waves. In 1988 I wrote a paper titled "Confusion in Camelot." This paper was about the unreported sins of the John F. Kennedy administration. An ABC television production in 1997 on the Kennedy administration covered the same ground I had done nine years earlier. In the introduction written in 1986 I thought it important enough to report the discovery of hidden Bible codes in the Old Testament with the use of computers. In 1997, eleven years later, the publishing market was flooded with books on hidden coded messages in the Bible. In 1979 I participated in a series of radio programs about the ashes of the red heifer in Israel to resume Temple worship services. It seems that everyone thought I was crazy, but in 1997 every major magazine, newspaper, and television news outlet in the world was reporting about the birth of an acceptable red heifer in Israel.

This does not mean that God is revealing to us privately about things that are to shortly come to pass. However, one of the spiritual gifts is the discernment of the Word of prophecy in the Bible. And it should be particularly noted that in the introduction I wrote in 1986 I noted specifically the possibility of every main computer in the world shutting down. Suddenly, here in 1998, almost without warning, we are informed by the most expert computer technicians in the world that this could literally happen on January 1, 2000 A.D. Why? Because of what is called the Millennium Bug, or the Y2K problem. World leaders are also becoming greatly concerned. What if you woke up on January 1, 2000, and there was no water coming out of your faucets; your electricity was cut off; you could not cash a check; there was no natural gas input to warm your house; wrecks were occurring because the traffic lights were out; your television and radio would not come on; there was rioting in the streets and thousands were rushing to the supermarkets to grab what available food stocks were available; you finally get to the service station to get enough gas to get to the airport to catch a plane to fly to another city to be with your parents, but there is no gas because the pumps won't come on because the electricity has been cut off; having just barely enough gas to get to the airport, you find that airplanes are not flying anyway because all the airplanes and airport computers are down. And, what about medical services? There probably will not be any.

Many will say that this cannot happen. Perhaps so. Maybe at the last minute someone will find the silver bullet, but time is short and experts say that we should not count on it. After a study on the Y2K problem, the *Daily Oklahoman* of June 24, 1998, reported that the only ones the Y2K problem will not affect will be those who have moved to another planet. The June 24, 1998, edition of *USA Today* reported that Speaker of the House Newt Gingrich has said that on January 1, 2000, there is going to be the greatest wreck the world has ever witnessed.

The main objective of this book by Dr. Larry Spargimino and myself is to present the evidence and let the readers determine for themselves their own response.

PART I

one

How Did We Get Into This Mess?

A CNN Internet item dated June 13, 1998, reported:

> WASHINGTON (AP)—The nation's power utilities told a Senate panel that they are working to solve the millennium computer problem. But they can't guarantee the lights won't go out on January 1, 2000. One utility didn't know how many lines of computer code it had, making it impossible to know how difficult or time-consuming its problem will be to solve with fewer than 18 months remaining. Sen. Chris Dodd, D.-Connecticut, said, "We're no longer at the point of asking whether or not there will be any power disruptions, but we are now forced to ask how severe the disruptions are going to be."

A Prodigy report dated June 15, 1998, quoted Senator Robert Bennett (R-Utah), chairman, Senate Special Committee on the Year 2000 Technology Problem: "In the event of a Y2K induced breakdown of community services, that might call for martial law."

The preceding Prodigy item continued to cite government sources indicating that in the event martial law would be necessary as a result of the Y2K problem, then military personnel might take over food distribution, communications, and transportation. Of course, under martial law constitutional rights would be voided. An August 29, 1994, Department of the Army directive outlined plans for using army camps as civilian prison camps. Item "C" of the directive specifically states: "Procedures for preparing requests to establish civilian prison camps on installations." A worldwide disruption of travel, communications, and transportation could result, not only in a national military dictatorship, but also a universal control authority. Farfetched? Possibly, but it is being proposed as a contingency.

But How Did the Y2K Debacle Come About?

In 1944 in the South Pacific I was told to connect a large cable from my radar unit to a large piano-like object on wheels. This object was called a "computer." It would receive information from my radar unit and convert it to firing data for our sixteen-gun antiaircraft battalion. Not only would the computer compute firing data faster, but infinitely more accurate. That was my introduction to a computer, and the following year two atom bombs were dropped on Japan.

We read in Genesis 1:3 that on the first day of creation God created light; on the second day of creation God made the firmament—one plus one equals two. On the third day God made the plants—two plus one equals three. Everything God made has a fixed numerical structure. Atoms have fixed numbers of neutrons, protons, and electrons. E equals MC^2 is a fixed mathematical equation that explains the numerical relationship between three universal elements. In music, art, metal, chemicals, etc., there are identifiable fixed mathematical properties. God indeed had to be a Master Mathematician to have created the heavens, the earth, and all things therein.

As the genesis computer models began the evolutionary process, these mathematical brains became smarter, faster, and more valuable. Satan promised Adam and Eve they could become smart enough to be their own god. Satan has never changed that lie because he hasn't had to; it works over and over. But Dr. Robert Jastrow, founder of the Goddard Space Flight Center, in his book *The Enchanted Loom*, projects that as the evolution of the computer progresses through the fifth generation stage it will attain godlike qualities, far surpassing the intellect of man himself who created it. In other words, the computer will be telling man what to do rather than the other way around. Should this be so, then man would have created his own god.

The June 30, 1980, edition of *Newsweek* (p. 50) carried an article titled "And Man Created the Chip." The inference, of course, is that God created man, then man created the chip, and thus man does not need God. The following is an excerpt from this article:

> A revolution is under way.... We are at the dawn of the era of the smart machine... an "Information Age" that will change forever the way an entire nation works, plays, travels, and even thinks. Just as the Industrial Revolution dramatically expanded the strength of man's muscles and the reach of his hands, so the smart-machine revolution will magnify the

power of his brain. But unlike the Industrial Revolution, which depended on finite resources such as iron and oil, the new Information Age will be fired by a seemingly endless source—the inexhaustible supply of knowledge itself. Even computer scientists who best understand the galloping technology and its potential, are wonderstruck by its implication. "It is really awesome," says L. C. Thomas of Bell Laboratories. "Every day is just as scary as the day before."

The driving force behind the revolution is the development of two fundamental and interactive technologies—computers and integrated circuits. Today, tiny silicon chips half the size of a fingernail are etched with circuitry powerful enough to book seats on jumbo jets, keep the planes working smoothly in the air, help children learn to spell and play chess well enough to beat all but the grandest masters. The new technology means that bits of computing power can be distributed wherever they might be useful.... This "computational plenty" is making smart machines easier to use and more forgiving of unskilled programming. Machines are even communicating with each other. "What's next?" asks Peter E. Hart, director of the SRI International artificial-intelligence center. "More to the point, what's not next?"

On the front cover of the June 30, 1980, edition of *Newsweek* appeared a computer screen with the readout, "Hello, I am your friend Chip. I'm getting smarter all the time. Soon I will be everywhere. And by my instant calculations society will never be the same."

The imagined and boastful predictions of Mr. Chip

have certainly been realized to a degree. Imbedded chips, by the billions upon billions, are now implanted in computer systems around the world. The problem is that several billion of these chips have a genetic and fatal flaw that will be revealed to the world on January 1, 2000, if not before.

On the way to making man a god in his own image, we once more refer to Dr. Robert Jastrow, director and founder of NASA's Goddard Institute for Space Studies. *Time* magazine in its February 20, 1978, edition, in an article titled "Toward an Intelligence Beyond Man's," quoted Dr. Jastrow as follows:

> As Dr. Johnson said in a different era about ladies preaching, the surprising thing about computers is not that they think less well than a man, but that they think at all. The early electronic computer did not have much going for it except a prodigious memory and some good math skills, but today the best models can be wired up to learn by experience, follow an argument, ask pertinent questions, and write pleasing poetry and music.
>
> They can also carry on somewhat distracted conversations so convincingly that their human partners do not know they are talking to a machine.
>
> ...As computers get more complex, the imitation gets better. Finally, the line between the original and the copy becomes blurred. In another 15 years or so ...we will see the computer as an emergent form of life. The proposition seems ridiculous because, for one thing, computers lack the drives and emotions of living creatures. But when drives are useful, they can be

programmed into the computer's brain, just as nature programmed them into our ancestor's brain as a part of the equipment for survival. For example, computers, like people, work better and learn faster when they are motivated. Arthur Samuel made this discovery when he taught two IBM computers how to play checkers. They polished their game by playing each other, but they learned slowly.

Finally, Dr. Samuel programmed in the will to win by forcing the computers to try harder—when they were losing. Then the computers learned very quickly. One of them beat Samuel and went on to defeat a champion player who had not lost a game to a human opponent in eight years. Computers match people in some roles, and when fast decisions are required in a crisis, they often outclass them....

We are still in control, but the capabilities of computers are increasing at a fantastic rate, while raw human intelligence is changing slowly, if at all.

Computer power is growing exponentially; it has increased evolution—vacuum tubes, transistors, simple integrated circuits, and today's miracle chips—followed one another in rapid succession, and the fifth generation, built out of such esoteric devices as bubble memories and Josephson junctions, will be on the market in the 1980s.

The article continues to relate that a man and a computer in the future can so work together that something will be produced that will be beyond human intelligence. Once more it is evident that Satan is still attempting to make good his promise to Eve that she and Adam would become as gods if they would eat of the tree of knowledge. Recently on national television a movie was shown where computers rebelled against their human partners, killed the leaders, and put computerlike replicas in their places. Then the human race became slaves of the computers. According to Dr. Jastrow's article, such a fantasy could at some future time become reality.

Let us remember that this article in *Time* magazine appeared twenty years ago. Twenty years ago computers were being programmed and trained to play checkers. Today, computers are playing and beating the best chess players in the world. Chess is the most mentally challenging game in the world. Some expert chess players have to think at least ten moves ahead. To improve mental toughness, every high school student should take up chess.

Let us suppose that Adam was created with brain power equal to that of a scientist today holding a doctor's degree, and we believe that he was. Let us also suppose that God gave Adam a problem to work concerning the relativity of time, space, and matter. On January 1, 1999, Adam rushes into our space center waving a paper with the answer he has just arrived at after almost six thousand years. A girl at a computer takes the same problem to check the answer, and in just thirty seconds she turns to Adam and verifies his answer. This is how fast the modern computer has speeded up scientific knowledge: six thousand years compared to thirty seconds. To illustrate further computer evolution, we refer to an article in the June 17, 1985, edition of *Time* about the Cray-2:

Software Manager Dieter Fuss stared at the message

and interpreted it for the assembled Livermore technicians and executives: "It just came alive and said: I'm ready." In that moment, a new era of high-speed computing began. The Cray-2 has the world's largest internal memory capacity (2 billion bytes) and a top speed of 1.2 billion FLOPS (floating point, or arithmetical operations per second), six to twelve times faster than its predecessor, the Cray-1, and 40,000 to 50,000 times faster than a personal computer. It outdistances the world's half-dozen other super-computer-machines especially designed to carry out vast numbers of repetitive calculations at incredible speeds—and is expected to make short work of problems that have vexed scientists and engineers for decades. Says Robert Borchers, Lawrence Livermore's associate director for computations: "What took a year in 1952 we can now do in a second." Who needs such blinding speed? ... U.S. intelligence agencies depend on supercomputers to sort through the enormous quantities of surveillance data beamed home by ground-based listening posts and orbiting spy satellites. By using supercomputers to simulate explosions, nuclear weapons experts require fewer test explosions to validate their designs. Machines like the Cray-2 are essential to any Star Wars defensive system for locating and intercepting incoming missiles before they re-enter the atmosphere.

In 1997 we were near the huge government scientific complex at Livermore, approximately twenty miles east of San Francisco. Poor Mr. Cray-2 was being replaced so soon by a more modern computer monolith.

The properties of God have been defined as follows:

Omnipotent: all-powerful
Omniscient: all-knowing
Omnipresent: everywhere

In Computer World, the computer is indeed all-powerful. No major business today can exist in national or international markets without a computer. Governments, science, utilities, communications, transportation, space programs, etc., operate only through the grace and mercy of computers and computer programmers.

In Computer World, computers are all-knowing, to the extent that all the information and knowledge about any item or entity, past or present, can be found on the Internet. How to split an atom, make a bomb, bake a cake, who killed Cock Robin, or how far it is from Gotebo to Timbuktu. Trillions of scientific, historical, geographical, archaeological, medical, or general information from the books of men who lived from Nimrod to Bill Clinton are available with the flick of a computer switch. The computer is all-knowing in the sense that it knows:

Your financial transgressions
Your legal transgressions
Your marital transgressions
In everything you do, like Santa Clause, it knows whether you've been good, or bad.

The computer is omnipresent in that every time you use a credit card, it knows where you are. In your tax returns, your social security card, your drivers license, your credit ratings, it knows your identity and contemporary circumstances. On thousands of mailing lists the computer data bank also keeps track of you. In sending out mailings at Southwest Radio Church ministries, we have to get a computer update from the government data bank on a quarterly basis. Below is the computer code mark identifying our general manager, Bob Glaze, and his present address. If Bob Glaze's name is omitted, the marks will get the letter to his home.

```
161711   W
BOB GLAZE

Oklahoma City OK  73127-3229
||..|..||....||..|.||...|..||...|.|..|.||.|....||...||..|.||
```

Whether you like it or not, you have a mark and a number in the government's computer data bank.

Mankind has stumbled into the amazing modern world much like Alice stumbled into her Wonderland. The world of today is just as different from the world of A.D. 1900 as Alice's dream world was from the world of reality. Just a few decades ago it was easier to believe in Alice's talking rabbit or the Queen of Hearts than a talking machine. Yet today, men and women talk to computers almost every day. There is now a computer program that will instantly translate spoken words, in any language, into printed words.

A Hebrew prophet by the name of Daniel wrote: "But thou, O Daniel, shut up the words, and seal the book even to the time of the end: many shall run to and fro, and knowledge shall be increased."

We are certainly living in the time of the end. Millions are running to and fro on the earth and through the air. Knowledge has increased in quantum leaps. Like Satan promised, we have eaten of the forbidden fruit of the knowledge of good and evil, and we have made gods in our own image. God himself has said that anything we can imagine, we can do (Gen. 11:6). So, what is all this talk about a Y2K computer glitch that may destroy our castles that will reach into the heavens? How could this possibly happen?

Because man is not God:

"For all have sinned, and come short of the glory of God" (Rom. 3:23).

"There is none righteous, no, not one: There is none that understandeth, there is none that seeketh after God. . . . There is none that doeth good, no, not one" (Rom. 3:10–12).

"Pride goeth before destruction, and an haughty spirit before a fall" (Prov. 16:18).

"For the wisdom of this world is foolishness with God. For it is written, He taketh the wise in their own craftiness" (1 Cor. 3:19).

"Professing themselves to be wise, they became fools, . . . And even as they did not like to retain God in their knowledge, God gave them over to a reprobate mind, . . . Backbiters, haters of God, despiteful, proud, boasters, inventors of evil things, disobedient to parents, Without understanding, covenantbreakers, without natural affection, implacable, unmerciful" (Rom. 1:22, 28, 30–31).

Surely that old man called Noah out there building an ark for one hundred and twenty years preparing for a flood must have been crazy? But he wasn't.

Surely God would not allow those mean old Romans

to destroy the beautiful House of the Lord on Mt. Moriah, glistening with gold and diamonds? But He did.

Surely man would be smart enough not to allow two world wars in one generation that would lay nations desolate and kill over one hundred million? But he wasn't.

And surely our great men of science and technologies would be wise enough not to omit two little spaces in the date field in computer programs that could adversely affect every man, woman, and child on planet Earth? BUT THEY DID!

Why? "For this is good and acceptable in the sight of God our Saviour; Who will have all men to be saved, and to come unto the knowledge of the truth. For there is one God, and one mediator between God and men, the man Christ Jesus: Who gave himself a ransom for all ..." (1 Tim. 2:3–6).

Here is an example of what programmers are faced with:

```
DETAIL-LINE-OUT.
 05 FILLER                   PIC X(01)          VALUE SPACES.
 05 DL-CUSTOMER-NAME-OUT     PIC X(25).
 05 FILLER                   PIC X(02)          VALUE SPACES.
 05 DL-NEW-PRINCIPAL-OUT     PIC $9,999,999.99.
 05 FILLER                   PIC X(05)          VALUE SPACES.
 05 DL-YEAR-PROCESSED-OUT    PIC 9(02).
 05 FILLER                   PIC X(85)          VALUE SPACES.
```

Diagram 1

```
                  INVESTMENT RESULTS
CUSTOMER                    PRINCIPAL         YEAR
XXXXXXXXXXXXXXXXXXXXXXXXX   $9,999,999.99      99
                            $9,999,999.99      99
                            $9,999,999.99      99
                            $9,999,999.99      99
                            $9,999,999.99      99
XXXXXXXXXXXXXXXXXXXXXXXXX   $9,999,999.99      99
                            $9,999,999.99      99
```

Diagram 2

Diagram 1 contains an actual COBOL program. Diagram 2 is the "output" end result of the program in Diagram 1.

Diagram 1 is a short computer program designed to calculate the principle of an investment account. Diagram 1 shows that 25 spaces have been set aside for the customer's name, indicated on the line labeled: "05 DL-CUSTOMER-NAME_OUT PIC X(25)." The output ot end result of the command is shown in Diagram 2 as:

CUSTOMER
XXXXXXXXXXXXXXXXXXXXXXXXX

If the cusomter's name is longer than this, it will be truncated.

The Y2K **culprit** is located in Diagram 1. Notice the line that reads: "05 DL-YEAR-PROCESSED_OUT PIC 9(02)." Only two (02) spaces are reserved for the last two digits of the year. Had four spaces been reserved, there would be no Y2K problem.

This program is typical of millions of programs that need to be fixed.

two

What Others Say About the Problem

Investigative research can be time-consuming. Researching the Y2K problem, however, is especially demanding because of the sheer volume of material that has been appearing on the subject. This is the book that had to be written because no one can logically ignore a topic that repeatedly keeps coming up in newspapers, magazines, special reports, and television documentaries.

But is it just a lot of hype? Let the reader be the judge. But remember, it's not just the prophecy buffs and doomsday alarmists that are talking about the Millennium Bug. In this chapter we want to present to our readers some of the latest information on the Y2K problem.

True Or False?

The European (October 16–22, 1997) featured a special entitled: "Millennium Prophecies—True or False?" It gave "true" to the following:

- The Pentagon has said that some of their missiles "may go haywire on 1 January 2000."
- Mikhail Gorbachev has warned American senators that

the millennium problem could cause serious problems for Russian nuclear power stations.
- The Year 2000 programme manager for the British Ministry of Defence likened the scale of the problem to "mounting a combined military exercise continually for the next three years."
- The former head of the British government's task force has warned the millennium problem could lead to riots in the streets.
- Four airlines have said they will not fly over the millennium to prevent their planes from crashing.
- Satellites could fail, leading to the collapse of international phone links.
- A British government minister has said pensions won't be paid and one hundred years of interest could be added to credit card balances.

The implications are staggering: Potential problems are anticipated for every area of our existence.

Planning for What You Are Not Sure Might Happen
The problem must be dealt with. But what kind of planning will work? Planning for this computer "crash" is tricky. No one knows exactly *what* will happen and *when* it will happen. Everyone has heard that the big day is January 1, 2000. However, the actual failure date depends on several variables. Some programs are year-end programs, others month-end programs. In other words the Millennium Bug may make its appearance at different times.

Beth Belton, writing in *USA Today* (June 24, 1998) reports that according to Rep. John LaFalco, D-New York, "major domestic and international glitches can occur at many points from April 9, 1999, to December 31, 2001." April 9, 1999, becomes "9999" on some computer programs. But "9999" also means "end of data file" and could permanently close files on that day. September 9, 1999, would create the same kind of "9999" error with the identical effect.

Complicating the Picture . . .

These and other factors greatly complicate the picture. Prodigy Online (March 13, 1998) reports that the introduction of the Eurodollar as the new, all-Europe currency on January 1, 1999, will create an almost unlimited number of new problems. ATM's all across Europe will need to be upgraded, and every business will need to make software changes to handle sales, currency exchanges, and taxes. Even if these technical problems can be remedied, the best computer programmers will be unavailable to deal with the Eurodollar changes because they are trying to deal with the Millennium Bug.

In addition to the changes generated by the introduction of the Eurodollar, other agencies are anticipating changes. The *Daily Oklahoman* (December 22, 1997) reported: "The IRS faces a huge job reprogramming its computers to reflect changes brought by the 1997 Taxpayer Relief Acts. . . . With all this work ahead, the IRS faces the unwelcome headache of keeping its computer programmers from jumping ship to more lucrative private jobs."

Caspar W. Weinberger, writing in *Forbes* (April 20, 1998) reports on the problem of a shortage of skilled programmers to adequately deal with the problem and the drain on finances:

> The worst of all the cataclysmic effects of the Y2K problem is that we will need all the available skilled manpower we have (with more hastily recruited...). Thousands of companies that have been planning to upgrade and improve all their systems in the next few years will have no money to do so....

Technical know-how is not the real problem. The real problem is finding the problem. *USA Today* (June 10, 1998) uses the analogy of fixing a bad rivet in the Golden Gate Bridge. Before you can fix a broken rivet in the Golden Gate Bridge you first have to find it. Computer software can have literally millions of lines of codes, requiring programmers to go over an unbelievably large volume of material.

What About the Lawsuits?

Why would nice people sue? When nice people don't get their pension checks, or get insurance payments in the wrong amount—like $2.50 instead of $2,500.00—nice people are no longer so nice.

The thing about lawsuits is that they are expensive, time-consuming, and aggravating. Reuters Online, updated May 7, 1998, reported: "A California legislative committee defeated a bill that would have immunized California software firms from lawsuits related to the millennium bug." Assemblyman Brooks Firestone introduced a much-needed bill in an attempt to protect software firms from "jackpot settlements" that would entice lawyers into litigation proceedings. "The bill would have exempted software firms and related computer companies from 'millennium bug' lawsuits claiming fraud, negligence, or unfair business practices, provided that the companies took reasonable steps to make their programs comply."

Lawsuits are sometimes the result of people getting mad. Not just angry, but mad. The following appeared in *Newsweek* (June 2, 1997). Do you think it might make you want to sue someone?

> Drink deep from your champagne glass as the ball drops in Times Square to usher in the year 2000. Whether you imbibe or not, the hangover may begin immediately. The power may go out. Or the credit card you pull out to pay for dinner may no longer be valid. If you try an ATM to get cash, that may not work either. Or the elevator that took you up to the party ballroom may be stuck on the ground floor. Or the parking garage you drove into earlier in the evening may charge you more than your yearly salary. Or your car might not start. Or the traffic lights may be on the blink. Or, when you get home, the phones may not work... your government check may not arrive, your insurance policies may have expired...

Why the Y2K Problem Is Not in the Realm of "Science Fiction"

It would be comforting if all of this were impossible, but our world's growing dependence on the computer makes it all strangely real. The *Baltimore Sun* (December 14, 1997) stated:

> Soon the federal government will never again prom-

ise 'the check's in the mail.' . . . On January 2, 1999, the federal government plans to begin making almost all its payments except tax refunds electronically, mostly through direct deposits. Already, more than half of the one billion payments the government makes each year—to federal employees, vendors, and beneficiaries, such as Social Security and Supplemental Security Income recipients—are made electronically, and the pace is accelerating.

Since July 26, 1996, when by law all payments to new recipients with bank accounts had to be made electronically, eighty-five percent of new social security beneficiaries have signed up for direct deposit. Sending money electronically is faster, cheaper, and more reliable than mailing checks. . . . An electronic transfer costs the government about two cents; sending a check costs forty-three cents. Making all payments electronically is expected to save the government $100 million a year. . . . Replacing wayward checks—and the government replaces more than 800,000 checks a year that were lost, stolen, delayed, or destroyed—often takes two weeks. Missed electronic transfers can be repeated within a day.

Society's increasing dependence on the computer can be attributed to our attraction to things that are convenient. Direct deposits and electronic transfers are convenient. They save the government money and solve the problem of lost or stolen checks. I, Larry, used to work for the New York City Welfare Department as a caseworker. Some of our biggest hassles came from situations in which clients had not received their checks. Computers solve the problem. But, in this case, the solution (our increasing dependence on the computer) is setting the stage for what could be the greatest ordeal the human race has ever experienced.

The Titanic Sinks Again

Edward Yardeni, chief economist at Deutsche Bank Securities, sees the Y2K problem as the *Titanic*. As reported in *USA Today* (June 10, 1998), Yardeni stated: "Everyone said the *Titanic* was the wonder of the age back then, and it was." He observed that many scientists believe that the *Titanic* sunk because of brittle, defective rivets—the smallest component of a seemingly unsinkable ship. Yardeni believes that "today's computers are the rivets of our booming economy."

According to Yardeni, some businesses are dragging their feet in dealing with the problem and therefore the federal government must step in to guide these businesses that are apparently ignoring the problem. Yardeni believes that government needs "to put a lot of pressure on those midsize companies to get their act together.... All you need is a couple of vital links in the entire global information network to fail, and the whole thing starts falling apart."

Having the government "put a lot of pressure" on anyone sounds dangerous, doesn't it? Is such a draconian solution farfetched? Apparently not. George Surdu, Ford Motor Company's global Y2K manager, is quoted in *USA Today* (June 10, 1998) as calling for SWAT teams: "We're taking a look at what we need to do to the (lagging) suppliers. It might result in the establishment of SWAT teams to come and help them, but that's not been decided yet."

Could the Y2K problem be the catalyst that establishes a one-world government? The justification: averting a worldwide computer meltdown. In order to protect society from what more and more believe will precipitate a worldwide disaster affecting everything from pension checks to utilities and nuclear missiles, individuals, businesses, and even nations will be pressured to become year 2000 compliant. Such a scenario would destroy an already-eroded American sovereignty. And the response could very well be: "Who cares about American sovereignty? I want my electricity back on."

The problem is so urgent that Rep. Stephen Horn, chairman, Subcommittee on Government Management, Information, and Technology, issued a "U.S. Federal Government Year 2000 Survey," dated July 30, 1996. This document provides a sample letter to be used in writing to various organizations such as:

- police department and sheriff's department
- water and sewer company
- the banks that issued your credit cards
- any institution that owes you money such as:
    banks where you have an account
    pension fund
    local insurance agency
    money market fund
    mutual funds
- the college that keeps your academic records
- the companies that keep your employment records
- companies that supply you with goods or services

The following are segments from this sample letter:

Dear ...:

I'm concerned about something I have been reading about in the press. It's a real problem: the disruption of computers beginning on January 1, 2000. This is sometimes called the Millennium Bug: "2000" is entered as "00." Computers recognize this as 1900 instead of 2000.

What I need to know is this: Has your organization had all of its mainframe computer codes repaired? Second, have all of your computer systems (including the programs on PC desktop computers) been certified year 2000 compliant . . . ?

Or, if your organization is not yet compliant, but has hired programmers who are now repairing the code, let me know.

If you're not the person I should be writing to, please let me know to whom I should write.

I want to be sure that I'm in no way dependent on suppliers that are dependent on a code that may crash in the year 2000. . . . The threat of a crashing domino effect is real. I don't want to get hit. I think you can understand my concern.

Sincerely yours,

The Extent of the Problem

The clock is ticking and the year 2000 draws nearer. Is this the date that will bring unprecedented madness and mayhem? How extensive is the problem? Will it affect you? Jon Denton, staff writer for the *Daily Oklahoman* (June 21, 1998), raises the question: "Should I Worry?" His answer:

Not if you don't have a computer, use machines no more complicated than scissors, and never depend on somebody else to deliver food or fuel or medical care. In other words, you have no problem with Y2K only if you live on another planet.

Is Jon Denton correct in his portrayal of the extent of the problem? The following is a brief survey of some of the areas that will probably be affected. The reader is encouraged to come to his, or her, own conclusions regarding the extent of the problem.

In a news conference on July 15, 1998, President Clinton emphasized the government's willingness to help employers needing programmers to "fix" their computer programs to be year 2000 compliant. A web site has been established by the U.S. Department of Labor (*www.dol.gov*). Employers looking for programmers have been encouraged to post their needs on that site. We checked the U.S. Department of Labor web site and found literally thousands of needs posted. For example, under the letter "A" alone there are sixty-four pages of companies needing help. With approximately fifty entries per page, that makes some thirty-two hundred companies needing help, and that's only for the first letter of the alphabet! This suggests the seriousness of the problem.

Medical Services

It's comforting to know that health care workers are prepared to deal with emergencies, but are they ready to cope with the Y2K emergency? Susan Parrott, writing for the *Daily Oklahoman* (June 25, 1998), states: "The so-called Year 2000, or Y2K, computer problem could wipe out thousands of devices used to diagnose and treat illness, along with hardware and software programs essential to business operations."

Transportation
The airlines are heavily dependent on computers to record ticket reservations, schedule flights, stay abreast of changing weather conditions, and for air traffic control—all vital in a day of crowded skies and rising airline ticket sales.

Automobile manufacturers depend on computers to run factory machines, order parts, and establish manufacturing schedules. UPS, FedEx, and other shipping companies use computers to track parcels and schedule flights and truck fleets.

Finance and Commerce
Retailers are dependent on computers to keep up with their stock and to insure that items are readily available in stores and outlets. Computers help in the management of warehouses and distribution centers.

Prodigy personal services posted January 21, 1998, cites one economist who warns of a forty percent chance of a serious global recession. "Even if the U.S. licks its computer glitch, other nations probably won't. A berserk computer overseas could easily gunk up the works here, sending stock markets plunging, drying up bank loans, and scaring off prospective merger partners."

The Millennium Bug will hit Canada as well. The *Toronto Star* (December 9, 1997) reported that "only one in ten Canadian companies is seriously tackling" the year 2000 problem. "Small firms with less than five employees have been slowest to address the issue with only six percent adopting formal action plans."

Some banks have launched an awareness campaign to educate their customers about the Y2K problem. BankFirst of Knoxville, Tennessee, has sent out a brochure on the year 2000 problem to its commercial account holders. The following was included in the cover letter:

> Whether your business is large or small, this issue is one that directly and/or indirectly affects the entire business community as well as society at large. The key to limiting the damage to your business, either by your own computer system or by others, is to begin dealing with it now, if you haven't already.

Clearly BankFirst believes that the Y2K problem will do some "damage." In fact, it's not a question of whether or not there will be "damage," but rather, how to limit "the damage to your business." The brochure has a paragraph titled "How Do Year 2000 Issues Affect My Organization?" The answer given:

> Year 2000 issues affect all programs that use dates. These might include the systems that process your accounts payable/receivable, historical records, inventory maintenance, debt collection, or production operations. The mechanical systems in your building such as elevators, climate control systems, telephone systems, or alarm systems may also be affected. If left unresolved, these problems may disrupt the normal business operation of your organization.

Utilities

Power companies depend on computers for everything from monitoring radioactive leaks at nuclear facilities to mailing out electric bills. Trying to "fix" the Y2K problem will be a financial drain on many utility companies. *USA Today* (June 10, 1998) reported that the Nuclear Regulatory Commission has estimated that the nation's fifty-five utilities operating one hundred and five reactors will spend between three and ten million dollars to upgrade their systems. Because utility companies are dependent on one another "the utility that does a sloppy job coping with Year 2000 fixes can ruin the best efforts of a diligent power producer. The resulting power-grid problem could lead to blackouts."

Others agree with this gloomy prediction. CNN Interactive posted a report dated June 13, 1998, titled "Y2K Bug Could Turn Off the Lights in the United States." A survey by a Senate panel of ten of our nation's largest utilities providing electricity to fifty million people found that none has completed contingency plans. At a recent hearing Senator Chris Dodd, D-Connecticut stated: "We're no longer at the point of asking whether or not there will be any power disruptions, but we are now forced to ask how severe the disruptions are going to be."

Military

Perhaps the scariest part of the Y2K scenario concerns the military. Missiles carrying nuclear, chemical, and biological warheads are highly dependent on computers. The major powers of the world are heavily dependent on computer-based systems to monitor possible surprise attacks.

According to *Technology News* (May 5, 1998), "The United States is drawing up plans to keep Russia and others from being spooked into millennium bug-related 'nightmare' military scenarios, a top Pentagon official said." Because of heavy reliance on computer systems to monitor the activities of would-be aggressor nations, everyone may have "their finger on the trigger" should the anticipated computer crash take place. The report went on to voice a major concern: "Arms control experts questioned whether Russian commanders, in a pinch, would take at face value word from Washington that no attack was imminent if Moscow feared otherwise."

The problem is compounded by the fact that Russia is doing virtually nothing to prepare for the crisis. The *Dallas Morning News* gave a frightening report in its June 20, 1998, edition when it stated: "Russia's Atomic Energy Ministry will wait until 2000 to fix any computer glitches arising from the millennium bug." According to a CNN Interactive online report (June 17, 1998) titled "Russia Needs to Wake Up to Y2K Threat, Experts Say," both Russian business and military agencies have adopted a wait-and-see policy before doing anything.

On a CBS TV news report, aired on July 22, 1998, Deputy Secretary of Defense John Hamre referred to the Y2K problem and said: "I think it's an electronic El Niño." In that same report CBS news correspondent David Martin stated: "The millennium bug is a $3 billion nightmare. It lurks deep in the 25,000 computer systems the Pentagon depends on for everything from firepower to payroll." The CBS report went on to state: "If tomorrow were January 1, 2000, Navy computers would not be able to plan missions for the Tomahawk cruise missile."

Evidently the Millennium Bug is not a figment of an overactive imagination. It's a real problem that could cause some "nasty surprises," said Hamre.

Nasty surprises could mean losing track of spare parts or loss of computerized satellite photo archives. . . . The Pentagon has little choice but to spend $3 billion for a fix. Hamre is so worried about whether the Pentagon will be ready for the year 2000 that he may soon order a halt to all other work on weapons and computers until they are first rid of the millennium bug.

three

What Happens If It Happens?

Recently Ken Alibek, a biochemist, second in command of the Russian germ warfare effort, defected to the United States. Mr. Alibek appeared on various television programs, and articles by him and about him were carried in various magazines and newspapers. The February 25, 1998, edition the *New York Times* featured Col. Alibek on the front page warning about deadly new biological weapons the Russians have developed, and either given or sold the technology to nations like Iraq and Iran. German newspapers, as reported in a Prodigy item of March 9, 1998, claimed that Saddam Hussein had stockpiled such biological weapons in rebuilt Babylon in the belief that the United States would not bomb such an important archaeological site. Such viruses and germs, capable of killing millions within a few days, could be released on the windward side of cities, wiping out entire metropolitan areas like Chicago, New York City, or Los Angeles. Such weapons could be smuggled in through Mexico or Canada in airtight sealed containers, or even brought into the country in bodies of women.

Recently Pakistan and India tested new nuclear

weapons and there are still thousands of nuclear missiles ready to be fired in Russia, China, the United States, France, England, Israel, and up to thirty nations of the world. President Clinton proudly announced to the nation in a speech that was carried on all major television networks that Russian nuclear missiles were no longer pointed at the United States, and that United States' missiles were no longer pointed at Russia. But on a "Sixty Minutes" show, a Russian general and a U.S. general were both asked how long it would take to re-aim their intercontinental missiles. Both responded, "From three to five seconds."

A new book by Col. Stanslave Lunev, a Russian military intelligence agent, warns that the Russian government is now under the control of the Russian Mafia, and that assassination squads are being trained to kill the president, congressional leaders, and key army personnel, as well as exploding "suitcase nuclear bombs," blowing up communications and power stations. This book was released on July 2, 1998, and warns that in spite of peace talks and what has happened in the former Soviet Union, Russia is preparing for an inevitable war. And, on top of all this gloom and doom, we have these dire predictions about what is going to happen to the world on January 1, 2000, as a result of the Y2K problem.

A couple of years ago a movie was released in which a high army officer confronted a lesser officer with the line, "I can't tell you the truth because you can't handle the truth." God had a reason for telling Adam and Eve not to eat of the fruit of the tree of knowledge of good and evil. Man has now gotten all this knowledge, but man cannot handle this knowledge.

We read of this gloomy prophecy by Jesus Christ in Luke 21:25–26:

> And there shall be signs in the sun, and in the moon, and in the stars; and upon the earth distress of nations, with perplexity; the sea and the waves roaring; Men's hearts failing them for fear, and for looking after those things which are coming on the earth: for the powers of heaven shall be shaken.

If Jesus had left the state of the world at the end of the age right here, it would all seem rather hopeless, but He continued in verses 27 and 28:

> And then shall they see the Son of man coming in a cloud with power and great glory. And when these things begin to come to pass, then look up, and lift up your heads; for your redemption draweth nigh.

The Y2K problem is certainly an embarrassment to man because this little mistake was so silly to begin with, and now, as Jesus prophesied, there is great perplexity in all nations—we cannot control biological weapons, or nuclear weapons, and now Y2K. So let us consider just one of the things that will happen, if it happens. We refer to a Reuters news item of April 29, 1998:

> Federal Reserve governor Edward Kelly estimated on Tuesday that U.S. businesses must spend about $50 billion to prevent massive computer crashes in 2000. The Year 2000 problem will touch much more than just our financial system and could have temporary

adverse effects on performance of the overall U.S. economy as well as the economies of many, or all, other nations if it is not corrected, Kelly said in prepared testimony before the Senate Commerce Committee. ... The Fed can do little to offset any negative impact from the Year 2000 problem, Kelly said, though it will be prepared to help where it can. "We will, of course, be ready if people want to hold more cash on New Year's Eve 1999, and we will be prepared to lend to financial institutions through the discount window under appropriate circumstances or to provide needed reserves to banking systems. ... But there is nothing monetary policy can do to offset the direct effects of a severe Y2K disruption."

The Federal Reserve says that money cannot solve the problem, but in case of a run on the banks, which surely will occur, the Fed will be ready to pump cash back into the banks to keep them open.

The largest computer mogul in the world is Bill Gates of Microsoft. At first, Bill Gates indicated that he was not overly concerned, but an April 1998 Microsoft press release announced in a headline to a six-page instruction that Microsoft had now opened up a year 2000 resource center in the event that any of that company's millions of customers had trouble with the Y2K problem. In fact, Mr. Gates now says that it is a critical problem. Mr. Gates also announced that "Microsoft Products Can Be a Key Component in the Overall Year 2000 Solution." It is not unlikely that Mr. Gates would like to solve all the Y2K problems and take over all computer technologies, which just may happen.

An item in the July 7, 1998, edition of *USA Today* announced: "Breakthrough May Help Squish Y2K Bug." The article states that Allen Burgess of little-known Data Integrity woke up in the middle of the night and suddenly had this bright idea how he could speed up the process of finding and correcting the two-space date field that would cause the Y2K problem. He claimed that it would speed up the correction process something like thirty times; however, two months previously I suddenly woke up in the middle of the day and saw a similarly claimed solution by a firm in Australia. But this speedup program, according to *USA Today,* is still being tested by the Federal Aviation Administration, and may or may not help.

We quote from the June 8, 1998, edition of *Travel Weekly* from an article by Bill McFarlane:

> Ninety-five percent of companies we surveyed said either their systems were not Y2K compliant or that they did not know if they were. . . . Date and time encroach on every layer of a computer system: hardware, operating systems and their underlying BIOS support systems, applications, files, and screens. The failure of any single layer will cripple the entire system. The problem is reminiscent of the monster in the *Alien* movies: It is insidious and lurking in all sorts of places in all disguises, ready to surprise us. . . . The Gartner Group in Stamford, Conn., estimated the worldwide cost of the problem will be between $400 billion and $600 billion. It should come as no surprise that the larger reputable organizations undertaking compliance testing and conversions are operating at

full capacity through Y2K. The Y2K industry includes a growing number of independent programmers and consultants offering to undertake testing and conversions. However, I advise you to be suspicious of their claims or quotes. Rather, take the opportunity to review the cost of replacing the systems, as opposed to converting them.

So, even if some of the claims of independents that they have a solution or partial solution, there are warnings that this just cannot be done. Even if every line of code is corrected, there is still the billions of imbedded chips in almost every computer system. To quote just one other statistic from the Technology Association of America:

> Ninety-four percent of information technology managers see the Y2K computer issue as a "crisis"; 44 percent of American companies have already experienced Y2K computer problems; 83 percent of U.S. Y2K transition project managers expect the Dow Jones Industrial Average to fall by at least 20 percent as the crisis begins to unfold.

As we have considered the guesses from observers and technicians as to what could happen as a result of the Y2K problem, they generally fall into three categories:

Level Number One

a. There will probably be regional, sporadic utility service interruptions which may include electrical blackouts. Some of these service interruptions may last even a week. Without electricity, other utility services like water may also be in doubt. Homes using electricity for heating, or electricity to operate furnace fans and thermostats, may suffer. Even with electricity, some home appliances may not operate.

b. In areas where there may be electrical blackouts, water systems that have insufficient generator backups may also be affected. Service stations may not be able to operate gasoline pumps without electricity; banks may not be able to continue normal transactions, resulting in temporary inconveniences in checking procedures and cash withdrawals.

c. Shortages in certain food items at local grocery stores and supermarkets may occur as a result of transportation problems and storage inventories. Telephone and television interruptions may occur due to satellite transmission failures.

d. While most hospitals have backup electrical generator systems, there may be interruptions in medical services. Also, a decline of twenty to forty percent on the stock market may be expected.

In preparing for level number one aftereffects of the Y2K problem, it would be well to have a month's supply of food; lanterns and lantern fuel; wood, fuel oil, or plenty of blankets; and at least five hundred dollars in cash. There may be cases of pillaging, burning, robbery, and rape, as there are certain segments of the population that always welcome an opportunity to engage in lawless activities. If there are minimal Y2K aftereffects such as listed in level one, then problems should either be corrected or bypassed in from one to three months, with the social order gradually returning to normal.

Level Number Two

All the problems listed that may occur in level one would be doubled or tripled. Thousands and possibly millions would die of starvation or freeze to death. Martial law would be declared and national guard units would be mobilized. The army would take over all communications and transportation facilities. Without water available to fire departments, conflagrations would rage out of control. Gasoline would be either rationed or nonexistent. Home owners would possibly need firearms to protect themselves and their property, and a citizen's food supplies could be the cause of one's own death.

Already citizens preparing for a Y2K problem that would be comparable to level two are causing shortages in survival items like generators. There also may be shortages in dried foods like beans and rice as available stocks are quickly bought up. The effect on banking, the stock market, and the general economy would be too drastic to even contemplate. Some have projected that a level two Y2K disaster would require a period of up to three years to fix and return nations to a semblance of stability. How many millions or billions would die as a result of famine or violence would be only a guess.

Level Number Three

Practically all communications and transportation would cease. Military missiles, some possibly armed with nuclear devices, could go out of control. Nuclear power plants in Russia and the third world could experience meltdowns, filling the atmosphere with deadly atomic poisons. The military and police forces would be unable to control the pillaging and carnage, resulting in total anarchy with survival being a personal matter. With contaminated water sources, sanitation would be nonexistent and deadly diseases would spread throughout the population. It is upon such a world that the four horsemen of the apocalypse would ride across the planet.

Is any of the preceding going to happen? I don't know. *Could any of the preceding happen?* Yes! *Could all of the preceding happen?* Possibly! *Is there going to be martial law under which constitutional rights may be aborted?* Maybe! I refer to *Presidential Executive Order—Year 2000 Conversion—February 4, 1998:*

> The American people expect reliable service from their Government and deserve the confidence that critical government functions dependent on electronic systems will be performed accurately and in a timely manner. Because of a design feature in many electronic systems, a large number of activities in the public and private sectors could be at risk beginning in the year 2000. Some computer systems and other electronic devices will misinterpret the year "00" as 1900, rather than 2000. Unless appropriate action is taken, this flaw, known as the "Y2K problem," can cause systems that support those functions to compute erroneously or simply not run. Minimizing the Y2K problem will require a major technological and managerial effort, and it is critical that the United States Government do its part in addressing this challenge.
>
> Accordingly, by the authority vested in me as President by the Constitution and the laws of the United States of America, it is hereby ordered as follows:

Section 1. Policy. (a) It shall be the policy of the executive branch that agencies shall:

(1) assure that no critical Federal program experiences disruption because of the Y2K problem;

(2) assist and cooperate with State, local, and tribal governments to address the Y2K problem where those governments depend on Federal information or information technology or the Federal Government is dependent on those governments to perform critical missions;

(3) cooperate with the private sector operators of critical national and local systems, including the banking and financial system, the telecommunications system, the public health system, the transportation system, and the electric power generation system, in addressing the Y2K problem; and

(4) communicate with their foreign counterparts to raise awareness of and generate cooperative international arrangements to address the Y2K problem.

(b) As used in this order, "agency" and "agencies" refer to Federal agencies that are not in the judicial or legislative branches.

Section 2. Year 2000 Conversion Council. There is hereby established the President's Council on Year 2000 Conversion (the "Council").

How did the human race get itself into such an impossible fix? Because the human race has decided not to retain God in their knowledge, He is proving again that the wisdom of man is foolishness. The nations have made the computer their god. In just fifty years the computer has taken control of every governmental, social, military, and economic facet of human effort and endeavor. Computers now even appraise the physical condition of the elderly and infirm and report to the medical staff which patients are worthy of treatment. But even as man in his wisdom has invented and evolutionized the perfect machine, he overlooked two little spaces on the COBOL software program.

> Why do the heathen rage, and the people imagine a vain thing? . . . He that sitteth in the heavens shall laugh: the Lord shall have them in derision.
> —Psalm 2:1,4

I wonder if God is not laughing at the predicament of the world as the year A.D. 2000 dawns?

Even if the trillions of dollars are spent on correcting every line of computer code, it will not solve the problem. Billions of computer chips have the same error encoded, and how can every computer be serviced and checked to try to find the encoded chips? As General Wheeler of the Armed Services High Command reported this past month in the *Daily Oklahoman*, to fix the Y2K problem is an impossibility.

On June 27, 1998, I met with my Gideon Northwest Oklahoma City chapter. My chapter is composed mainly of business executives. One CEO who manages factories in Germany, India, and China, reported that on a recent return from Germany he sat next to another business executive. He asked this CEO next to him if his company was Y2K compliant. The response was that the Y2K hype was a lot of baloney. My Gideon friend then asked the other CEO if his company had stock listed on the exchange, and the reply was yes. Then my Gideon friend asked what the stock symbol was. The other CEO then asked if my friend wanted to buy some of his company's stock. At that, my friend remarked, "No, I just want to be sure that I don't buy any of your stock."

A few are now becoming aware of the possible consequences of the Y2K coming disaster. But why is it not being mentioned in the churches? Why are not more becoming concerned with the catastrophe that may lie just around the corner? The same reason that few prepare for death. We know that it is "appointed unto man once to die, and after that the judgment," but so very few want to think about death or discuss it. The same is to be applied to the Y2K problem. It could be so disastrous, so catastrophic, that the majority maintain the attitude of "eat, drink, and be merry, for tomorrow we die."

Out of the Y2K debacle, could there come a universal software program that would assign every individual an individual code mark and number? Some secular computer sources are even advocating this solution so that the present problem will never occur again.

> And he causeth all, both small and great, rich and poor, free and bond, to receive a mark in their right hand, or in their foreheads: And that no man might buy or sell, save he that had the mark, or the name of the beast, or the number of his name. Here is wisdom. Let him that hath understanding count the number of the beast: for it is the number of a man; and his number is Six hundred threescore and six.
> —Revelation 13:16–18

How can a man or woman escape from taking the mark of the beast? By receiving Jesus Christ as Lord and Savior now. Those who are saved by faith in Jesus Christ, as we believe the Bible affirms, will be taken out of the world before the mark of the beast arrives on the world scene.

four

The Y2K Problem and Bible Prophecy

It Fits Into the Prophetic Picture, Somewhere...
The world races toward the year 2000 and the beginning of the new millennium. What surprises are on the threshold of this new millennium?

Optimists, always looking for arguments to bolster their belief in the goodness of man and the upward climb of mankind, claim as proof the demise of communism, the thawing of the Cold War, the opening of doors in China, and a period of relative calm in the Middle East. Pessimists, however, need cite only one development to bolster their argument for a gloomy future: the Y2K problem.

The Y2K problem promises to bring untold suffering, confusion, and disruption to a society that has been pampered with modern conveniences. Some of the glitches already in evidence give us a preview of the devastation that could be caused by the Millennium Bug. *USA Today* (June 26, 1998) quoted Adrian Peracchio, a member of *Newsday*'s editorial board, as saying:

> Last year, the stock exchange in Brussels was shut

down for two hours because of Y2K-related problems with . . . the software. In those two hours, lost commissions totaled $1 million—and the problem was relatively minor and easily fixed. There have been already more than 10,000 similar—and similarly costly—Y2K instances reported in the United States alone.

Please note: one million dollars was lost in a two-hour computer crash in one stock exchange. What would happen if the computer crash was worldwide, as is anticipated, and lasted two days, or two weeks?

The above edition of *USA Today* also quoted the *Columbus Dispatch* to show the effects of another computer glitch:

> A tiny glimpse into the doomsdayers' future was provided last month when a communications satellite died and millions of people were thrown into panic when their cellular phones wouldn't operate; technology is great when it works and nearly satanic when it doesn't. . . .

God is not surprised by any of this because He is working according to His master plan. "Behold, the former things are come to pass, and new things do I declare: before they spring forth I tell you of them" (Isa. 42:9). The Y2K problem, therefore, fits into this plan and is part of that plan.

Prophecy helps us to understand the future but it also helps us to know where we are at present. We can't understand today unless we know about tomorrow. As we have seen, the newspapers and other forms of media are presenting us with new reports on the Y2K problem on a daily basis. How does it all fit together?

The following analogy may help. Think of the pieces of a jigsaw puzzle. They all appear to be unrelated and without meaning or place. How do those pieces fit together? It's hard to tell—unless you first look at the picture that is on the box *before* you start fitting the pieces together. By looking at the picture you can tell precisely how each piece fits.

The reports and write-ups dealing with the Y2K problem are the pieces of the jigsaw puzzle. The prophetic Scripture provides the picture. The Y2K problem doesn't make sense—until we see where God's Word says we are going.

From what has been presented and discussed relating to the Y2K problem, it is possible to discern several areas of prophecy where the Y2K problem could possibly fit in. Each of these areas bear a definite connection to the Y2K problem, a problem that will produce conditions conducive to the fulfillment of these prophecies.

Searching for a Connection

The Bible is the most amazing book of all because it has God as its author. It doesn't need to be corrected, updated, or revised because of new discoveries. And because it is timeless it always is relevant. It's hard to believe that the Bible does not say anything about the Y2K problem.

That's a faith-statement, but it is made more compelling because of the many prophetic signs that have appeared in the last fifty, or so, years. Large numbers of prophecies find their fulfillment in a time when Israel is in her land as an identifiable nation. For some two thousand years Israel was run and overrun by foreign nations, but on May 14, 1948, all of that changed when Israel became an independent state. The formation of the European Common Market, the European Union (EU), and the Eurodollar are also significant because they show that the stage is being set for the fulfillment of prophecies regarding the "reviving" of the Roman Empire.

The Counterfeit Millennium

Since Satan's original revolt against God, it is clear that Satan wants the authority and power of God. Long ago Satan said: "I will ascend above the heights of the clouds; I will be like the most High" (Isa. 14:14). Satan wants a worldwide kingdom, a counterfeit millennium. The new world order, with its one-world leader, the Antichrist, is this counterfeit millennium.

What could produce greater worldwide distress—no utilities, water, social security checks, ATMs, a worldwide financial depression, riots, famines, etc.—than the Y2K problem. The Y2K problem could very well produce a totalitarian police state of universal proportions *that will be welcomed by everyone*. Totalitarian regimes are always unpopular *unless* they are perceived as solving some common problem that can only be resolved by such drastic measures. Might the Y2K problem be that common problem? It will even have an effect on the IRS, as the following report from the *Daily Oklahoman* (December 22, 1997) indicates:

> At the Internal Revenue Service [fixing the Y2K problem] involves scouring 62 million lines of computer

code to ensure computers don't crash at the millennium. The estimated cost is $900 million, second to the Defense Department as the costliest Year 2000 fix in government. In addition, the IRS faces a huge job reprogramming its computers to reflect changes brought by the 1997 Taxpayer Relief Acts.... With all this work ahead, the IRS faces the unwelcome headache of keeping its computer programmers from jumping ship to more lucrative private jobs.

And what would happen if the average Mr. Taxpayer finds out that the IRS is having trouble keeping the books and keeping tabs on those who may be inclined to "fudge" on reporting their taxes? Will there be widespread cheating, and if there is, will the IRS adopt draconian measures to deal with the problem?

Since the 1995 tragedy in Oklahoma City many Americans have come to believe that the only solution to terrorism at home and abroad is increased surveillance and resultant loss of liberty. Airports have tightened security. Vehicles must not be left in front of the terminal, and passengers are required to show a picture ID. And yet no one minds. We want to feel "safe" no matter what the cost.

Satan's counterfeit millennium will produce worldwide bondage. The idea of a kingdom or millennial reign has implicit in it the idea of control. In the true millennium Christ shall rule "with a rod of iron" (Rev. 19:15). In the counterfeit millennium the Antichrist shall rule with a number—666:

And it was given unto him to make war with the saints,

> and to overcome them: and power [authority] was given him over all kindreds, and tongues, and nations. ... And he causeth all, both small and great, rich and poor, free and bond, to receive a mark in their right hand, or in their foreheads: And that no man might buy or sell, save he that had the mark, or the name of the beast, or the number of his name. Here is wisdom. Let him that hath understanding count the number of the beast: for it is the number of a man; and the number is Six hundred threescore and six.
> —Revelation 13:7, 16–18

Nimrod, the builder of Babylon, was the first world dictator (Gen. 10:8–10). During his reign, the descendants of those who survived on the ark attempted to build a tower to heaven, though God judged this first attempt at "globalism" by confounding their language and scattering them across the earth (Gen. 11:1–9). Later, others sought to dominate nations and peoples. Their attempts are prophesied in Daniel 2.

More recently the Illuminati, founded by Adam Weishaupt in 1776, carried the banner and sought to abolish structured government, private wealth, nationalism, and the family. Religion was to be replaced by reason. The Illuminati was tied in with the French Revolution, but was replaced with an organization having a broader agenda and influence in 1847 when Karl Marx formed the communist league.

Additional organizations with global designs have come on the scene, such as the Club of Rome and the United Nations. With rapid proliferation of weapons of mass destruction to small, unstable nations, cries have been ringing out across the world for the U.N. to step in and take control of the situation "for the good of all mankind."

The Y2K problem is another crisis situation. Because of the interdependence of utilities, banking, military, missile defense, and commerce, it is imperative that the whole world become year 2000 compliant. A chain is only as strong as its weakest link. Nations that refuse to spend the money (or can't) to become year 2000 compliant may be pressured in a variety of ways. Just as guilty global citizens can be fined for polluting the air or water, those who are not year 2000 compliant could be slapped with heavy fines and sanctions. There are a whole host of possibilities, but they all spell control and loss of sovereignty.

The Focus Is on Europe

Daniel 2:24–45 speaks about four empires: the Babylonian, the Medo-Persian, the Grecian, and the Roman. With the conquest of Sicily in 242 B.C. Rome quickly rose to a position of dominance in the ancient world.

Jerusalem fell to the Romans in 63 B.C., and by the time Christ was born the entire Mediterranean basin and beyond was under Roman jurisdiction. The Bible makes it clear, however, that Daniel's prophecy regarding Rome has not yet been completely fulfilled. It is in a period of ten Roman kings that the kingdom of God on earth is established:

> And in the days of these kings shall the God of heaven set up a kingdom, which shall never be destroyed: and the kingdom shall not be left to other people, but it

> shall break in pieces and consume all these kingdoms, and it shall stand for ever.
>
> —Daniel 2:44

It is often asserted that the Antichrist is of Jewish origin, but careful analysis of the relevant scripture texts throws that into question. Proponents of the Jewish origin idea argue that since the Jews will accept the Antichrist as their Messiah he must be Jewish because they would not accept a Gentile as their Messiah.

The fallacy of such reasoning is that just because the Jews are in a covenant with the Antichrist (Dan. 9:27) does not mean that they accept him as their Messiah. Other considerations also argue against his Jewish origin. For example, while Daniel 11 speaks of Antiochus Epiphanes, a Gentile, most premillennial commentators would say that Antiochus is a type of Antichrist. The Gentile origin of Antichrist, therefore, is strongly suggested by Bible typology. Furthermore, Revelation 13:1 and 17:15 picture Antichrist as rising out of the sea, a prophetic symbol for the Gentile nations of the world in turmoil.

Also significant in the discussion of the origin of the Antichrist is that Daniel 9:26–27 connects the origin of the Antichrist with a Gentile kingdom. The one confirming the covenant with Israel represents the Revived Roman Empire, since it was the Romans who destroyed the Jewish Temple in A.D. 70.

At any rate, Antichrist emerges from the sea and he appears on the scene in a time of confusion and dismay (Rev. 6:1–8). To say the least, the Y2K problem will throw the world into a tailspin. In fact, according to a report printed in the *Daily Oklahoman* (June 26, 1998), retired Brigadier General Ed Wheeler stated that the Y2K problem is "unsolvable." The report went on to state:

> Governments should follow military tactics when devising their wartime strategy, said the Tulsa resident [Gen. Wheeler] who led National Guard troops into the Persian Gulf crisis. "As a military commander, I would never commit all my troops to one line of defense," he said. "The civilians have all their eggs in one basket." That basket may unweave in 2000 when a much-publicized computer glitch takes effect.

The world has always searched for peace apart from God. People want the contentment and security of peace without the responsibilities of faith and repentance. The world will look for someone who promises to bring peace out of turmoil and confusion. The world is looking for someone who will do just that. Antichrist's actions will speak louder than words as he does the impossible.

With Europe coming more and more into the fore, it will have greater financial and military clout. Someone will need to bring a measure of control and stability to an unstable world. European leaders have seen the need to unite. The countries of Europe can no longer survive in a competitive world market if they have separate product standards and separate monetary policies.

<u>A central authority is necessary to establish unity and also to bring stability. Might Europe play the role of somehow policing the world in a world of confusion created by the Y2K problem?</u>

In 1902 President Theodore Roosevelt made this revealing statement to Congress: "More and more, the increasing interdependence and complexity of international politics and economic relations render it incumbent on all civilized and orderly powers to insist on the proper policing of the world" (John Blum, *The Republican Roosevelt*, pp. 824–825).

The confusion generated by the Millennium Bug may create a need for order and stability, and for a charismatic leader to unite the world. His leadership will be forceful and dictatorial, but he will have a massive following because bondage will be better than anarchy.

The New World Religion

The Scriptures speak about a new world order, and also about a new world religion. The Antichrist will receive universal worship and adoration (Rev. 13:4). In a context speaking of the great whore, Revelation 17:2 states: "With whom the kings of the earth have committed fornication, and the inhabitants of the earth have been made drunk with the wine of her fornication." Spiritual adultery is not generally used in Scripture of heathen nations that know not God, but rather of a people who outwardly carry the name of "God," or the name of "Christian," while denying its reality. This presents us with a picture of an alliance between the apostate church and the political powers.

The confusion created by the Millennium Bug will create a hunger for "religion," and the religion of the future will offer it.

Undoubtedly, the Y2K problem will be fixed at some point. We may ask, however, what will be the effect on the population of the world? Will it be universal adoration and worship as is predicted for the Antichrist?

Y2K and Armageddon

For they are the spirits of devils, working miracles, which go forth unto the kings of the earth and of the whole world, to gather them to the battle of that great day of God Almighty. . . . And he gathered them together into a place called in the Hebrew tongue Armageddon.

—Revelation 16:14, 16

Throughout the history of the human race there has been war. Untold millions of men, women, and children have been killed or maimed as a direct result of hostilities, and countless millions more have suffered and died because of the disruption that war always causes. One battle, however, outshines all others in significance and scope. It is known by Christian and non-Christian, believer and nonbeliever as Armageddon.

The continued rise of anti-Semitism, the aligning of nations against Israel, the existence of Islamic republics that have broken away from the Soviet Union and which possess weapons of mass destruction and the inclination to use those weapons, all fit in with what the Bible says about a coming war in the Middle East that will engulf the entire planet. But how does the Y2K problem fit into the picture?

The Y2K problem promises to pose a security risk. *USA Today* (June 25, 1998) reported that "the Year 2000 computer glitch could help adversaries penetrate critical U.S. businesses, government, and defense computers." CIA director George Tenet stated: "We are building an information infrastrucure, the most complex the world has ever known, on an insecure foundation." In seeking to "fix" the Y2K problem, companies and government agencies must open their computer systems, and that "provides all kinds of opportunities for someone with hostile intent" to plant viruses that would cripple the systems and gain highly sensitive information.

Computer hackers have successfully gotten access to sensitive information. An eighteen-year-old Israeli master hacker who calls himself "The Analyzer," hacked his way into U.S. computers and has vowed to pass on his hacking skills to others. Prodigy e-mail, posted March 12, 1998, states that the Computer Security Institute said "sixty-four percent of computer security specialists at U.S. companies, government agencies, banks, and universities, have reported security breaches within the last year."

Such breaches could encourage armed aggression by a foreign aggressor who thinks that he will be successful because of his knowledge of the enemy's defenses, and believes that he has the ability to cripple the enemy's ability to wage war.

Horses and Primitive Weapons

Bible commentators have discussed the prophetic Scripture's references to horses and primitive weapons in the battles of the future. Though there are some descriptions of worldwide devastation that could be produced by weapons of mass destruction, there are often statements indicating the usage of primitive weapons. For example, Revelation 14:20 speaks about blood rising "unto the horse bridles." Ezekiel 38:15 speaks of a mighty invasion force, "all of them riding upon horses." Is this literal?

Two solutions have been proposed. One says that

since the biblical authors thought in terms of their own society and culture, they described these future wars in terms that were familiar to them and their audiences. The other solution has been to say that these are literal horses and literal primitive weapons.

If this is the correct solution to the problem, the inevitable question would be: Why the usage of primitive weapons in the future? The Y2K problem may provide a possible answer: *Because modern weapons won't work.* Computer glitches may be so widespread that modern weapons simply will break down and not function.

Y2K and Globalism

U.S. News & World Report (October 24, 1994) reported that the yearly amount spent by the U.S. for national defense has been on the decrease for several years in a row. In 1990, our defense budget was $348.6 billion; in 1992, it was $310.8 billion; in 1994, $266.7 billion.

Any serious breach of national security could be devastating to our country. If America's military is further compromised, as it has been over the past several years, it might appear more feasible to join an international organization and put our defense in the hands of that organization. This would wipe out American sovereignty and make the nation a puppet state paying tribute to a global organization. Former Secretary of State Henry Kissinger painted a gloomy but accurate picture:

> We [the United States] are sliding toward a world out of control, with our relative military power declining, with our economical lifeline increasingly vulnerable

to blackmail, with hostile radical forces growing in every continent and with the number of countries willing to stake their future on our friendship dwindling.
—*Time*, April 21, 1980

Will We Be Able to "Tough It Out"?

What will it be like when millions in cities like Los Angeles and New York have no water and no electricity? What happens if it is a cold winter and there is no heat for days on end? How will people who are on prescription drugs fare when they can't get their medication?

It is clear that the Millennium Bug will probably impose unbelievable hardships on the human race, especially on those living in populated areas who are dependent on public utilities, transportation, supermarkets, and communications. Since most of us do not live in a remote jungle clearing and do not "live off the land," most of us fall in this category and will be seriously affected. The big question: Will we be able to cope? Will we be able to shrug off the danger and inconvenience and "tough it out"?

One of the factors that would militate against giving a "yes" answer to this is our society's increasing dependence on "feel good" drugs. Martin and Deidre Bobgan, in their *PsychoHeresy Awareness Letter* (Jan.-Feb. 1998) lament the fact that many children are being overmedicated and childhood behavior is being pathologized. Many childhood behavioral problems are being diagnosed under the category of "mental disorder." Consequently, drugs are being prescribed to take care of the problem. The Bobgans quote the *Wall Street Journal* (April 4, 1997) where it is reported:

> The makers of Prozac, Zoloft, Paxil, and other antidepressants are taking aim at a controversial new market: children. . . . Drug companies are racing to compile data on whether their drugs are safe and effective in children. . . . Drug-makers are also preparing medications in easy-to-swallow form that will be more palatable to even the youngest of tykes.

Antidepressants and other medications may make their users feel better and provide a temporary "lift," but, in the process, are they learning how to cope? If not, millions are being ill-equipped to face the most stressful situation ever faced by the human race.

The Anatomy of a Disaster

The Bible tells us that the end-times scenario will be characterized by unpreparedness—people ignoring warnings and carrying on business as usual. "For as in the days that were before the flood they were eating and drinking, marrying and giving in marriage, *until* the day that Noe entered into the ark" (Matt. 24:38).

Of course, not everyone believes that the Y2K problem will be as devastating as some are claiming it will be. For example, the *Sunday Oklahoman* (June 28, 1998) reports: "Utilities Expect to Stay Online as 2000 Arrives." And yet, on the same page, Oklahoma Representative Fred Perry voiced distrust of the standard explanation and promise given to concerned inquirers: "Yes, we know there is a problem. We have appointed a task force. We are working on it. We are sure we will solve it."

five

Tightening the Noose: Y2K and Universal Bondage

> The people never give up their liberties but under some delusion.
>
> —Edmund Burke, 1784

In Matthew 24:8 our Lord was speaking about woes that would come in the last days: "All these are the beginning of sorrows." "Sorrows" refers to a particular kind of sorrow, namely the pain that a mother in labor experiences. Our Lord is saying: "These are the beginning of birth pains."

In using this language the Lord Jesus Christ implies several things about the woes prophesied for the world. For one thing, birth pains are associated with a unique event: childbirth. The world has always had times of upset and disruption caused by wars, famines, floods and pestilence, but the sufferings described in the Tribulation passages of Scripture are uniquely associated with the cataclysmic judgments of the end times. Secondly, birth pains are irreversible and do not cease until the baby is born. The Tribulation woes are irreversible and will reach their full intensity as described in the Bible.

Is the Y2K problem included in this "beginning of sorrows"?

The Antichrist's Agenda: World Domination

Manipulation with a view to controlling the masses is the ultimate goal of the Antichrist. "And he shall confirm the covenant with many for one week [seven years]: and in the midst of the week [after three and one-half years] he shall cause the sacrifice and the oblation to cease . . ." (Dan. 9:27). After the Antichrist consolidates his power over ten Western nations [the Revived Roman Empire and possibly including the U.S.], he will rule for some three and a half years at the beginning of the Tribulation. Where does the U.S. fit into the picture? Some of the possibilities include:

- being taken over by the European Union;
- being destroyed in some kind of a sudden military attack launched either by a superpower or by well-equipped terrorists;
- collapsing because of internal problems, i.e., stock market crash, moral breakdown, social unrest, et al.;
- being rendered a puppet state and being subjugated by a world organization.

The Millennium Bug could accomplish any, or all, of the above.

Important Strands of Recent History

One does not really have to be a particularly astute observer of history to know that several elitist groups have been assuming more and more control of our nation. Two are especially prominent: the Trilateral Commission and the Council on Foreign Relations.

President Carter stacked his administration with fellow members of the Trilateral Commission. According to *U.S. News and World Report* (February 21, 1977):

> The "Trilateralists" have taken charge of foreign policy making in the Carter administration, and already the immense power they wield is sparking some controversy. Active or former members of the Trilateral Commission now head every key agency involved in mapping U.S. strategy for dealing with the rest of the world.

The CFR, or Council on Foreign Relations, is another organization with a similar agenda as that of the Trilateral Commission. During the last four decades the CFR has exerted considerable influence in both the Republican and Democratic administrations as evidenced by the fact that its members have occupied key positions in government. Included in its membership: Dwight Eisenhower, Adlai Stevenson, John F. Kennedy, Henry Cabot Lodge, Richard Nixon, Hubert Humphrey, George McGovern, Gerald Ford, Nelson Rockefeller, Jimmy Carter, Walter Mondale, Geraldine Ferraro, Michael Dukakis, George Bush, and Bill Clinton. In some of the elections, both presidential and/or vice presidential candidates in both major parties have been members of the CFR.

Globalist ideals also direct the educational establishment. The *NEA Journal* (January 1946) had an article by its editor, Joy Elmer Morgan, titled "The Teacher and World Government," in which it is stated:

> In the struggle to establish an adequate world government, the teacher... can do much to prepare the hearts and minds of children for global understanding and cooperation.... At the very top of all the agencies which will assure the coming of world government must stand the school, the teacher, and the organized profession.

Elitist groups have unilaterally taken upon themselves the prerogative of making changes of global significance, changes which abridge the liberties of billions of people without their consent. Fueled by socialistic ideologies these groups, totally out of sympathy with Christian values, have introduced widespread changes without debate, discussion, or an open forum. They are working under a shroud of secrecy, and the disruptions caused by the Y2K problem could be a staunch ally in their cause. The fact that Antichrist exalts himself and "that he as God sitteth in the temple of God, shewing himself that he is God" (2 Thess. 2:4) suggests he is seeking ultimate control of the world. God seeks to exercise control in our lives by our willful surrender to Christ as Lord. Antichrist will exercise control by demanding it.

"It can't be wrong because it promotes so much good..."

Many of these developments seem nonthreatening because of the good they accomplish. The socialists with their egalitarian agenda and global aspirations of putting an end to world strife have become the unsung heroes of our era. The *New York Times* featured a revealing editorial on May 11, 1992, titled "The Unsung New World Army." It stated:

> The army of tomorrow is neither the Red Army nor the U.S. Army. . . . If there is to be peace, it will be secured by a multinational force that monitors cease-fires . . . and protects human rights. Blue-helmeted United Nations peacekeepers are doing just that. . . .

The Drug Epidemic
The drug epidemic is currently ravaging America. In addition to the harmful effects of the drugs themselves, this plague has unleashed the greatest crime wave in history. However, the greatest casualty may be the loss of our individual liberties as local and national governments are using totalitarian police methods to deal with a problem so serious that most people are willing to surrender their liberties even on the hope that the problem may thereby find a solution.

Global Warming
The same can be said about global warming, the highly-touted "crisis" that the proponents of the New World Order are using to force nations to submit to international intervention. Variations in weather that have been in evidence over the past several years may simply be caused by variations in the natural weather cycle. However, the politically correct global-warming hypothesis attracts the fervent and impassioned support of those who advocate the dissolution of national sovereignty.

"The Rights of the Child"

During the tense period of confrontation with Iraq, President George Bush left Washington to join more than seventy other heads of state at the United Nations World Summit for Children. With heart-rending photographs of dignitaries hugging adorable little children and with cries of "save the children!" world opinion was united and all agreed that "something must be done."

The rhetoric was exhilarating to millions who wanted to know that they can make a difference. Who can find fault with saving children from abuse, torture and the worst forms of cruelty? The idea found immediate and universal acceptance, as the U.N.'s "Fact Sheet No. 10: The Rights of the Child" indicated:

> The Convention entered into force on 2 September 1990—one month after the twentieth State ratified it. ... A little over seven months separated the opening for signature and the entry into force of the Convention: this is a very short period for an international treaty—generally it takes much longer—and it shows the worldwide interest and support for the child Convention.

But should we all rejoice, or is there more here than meets the eye?

The United States Constitution and Bill of Rights protect individuals and local governments from intrusion. Unfortunately, the Convention on the Rights of the Child provides the authority for the U.S. government, acting under the auspices of the U.N., to enforce its provisions against local governments and even against individual parents. Does this not set the stage for draconian measures to be imposed on individuals by agencies who have not been elected by the people and who have not pledged their support of the United States Constitution?

Heroic Struggles to Maintain Sovereignty: Will They Prevail?

The state of Virginia recently challenged the authority of the World Court—and won. As reported in *World* (April 25, 1998), Secretary of State Madeleine Albright and the World Court pleaded with Governor Jim Gilmore that Paraguayan Angel Francisco Breard, sentenced to death for a 1992 murder and attempted rape, be spared. Gilmore refused and Breard, 32, who claimed "the devil made me do it," was executed by lethal injection. His last words: "Glory be to God!" Ms. Albright stated she feared the case would jeopardize the safety of Americans incarcerated in other countries.

In the final days before the execution, the fifteen-member United Nations Tribunal ruled that the execution be blocked. The basis of their ruling was that Virginia failed to notify Paraguay of Breard's arrest, something required by the Vienna Convention. The governor said he appreciated Ms. Albright's concern about the safety of Americans abroad, but stated that he was also concerned about the safety of Virginians who would be easy prey to murderers.

In a globalist setup, will this kind of thing be allowed?

On the Threshold of Martial Law: The Y2K Problem Could Push Us Over

"Martial law" (*lex martialis*) initially referred to the regulations enforced by the Court of the Constable and Marshal in medieval England. It is military rule exercised by a government over its own citizens in an emergency situation sufficiently grave to warrant such action. It may be imposed in wartime, or in any situation in which the government, because of public disorder or natural catastrophe, deems such stringent measures necessary for the well-being and stability of the nation. According to the *Encyclopedia Americana*, in European and Latin American countries, martial law is commonly referred to as "a state of siege." The term is derived from the practice of transferring all civil authority in a town or city that is under attack to a military commander.

What are the possible conditions that could be generated by the Y2K problem that may be deemed sufficiently grave as to be perceived as warranting a declaration of martial law?

Severe economic and financial upsets
People may decide to make a run on the bank, creating an economic collapse. *CIO* magazine, as reported on Prodigy, posted July 8, 1998, conducted a survey in which people without mainframe computer experience were asked: "What would you do if you thought the Millennium Bug threatened the banks?" A quarter of them replied: "Take my money out of my bank." This may be perceived as a highly rational response because:

1. It is doubtful if all banks will be year 2000 compliant.
2. If a bank should become compliant, the system will be in jeopardy every time it networks with other computers that are noncompliant.

3. Japanese banks are too pressed with the Asian banking crisis to devote sufficient funds to fixing their Y2K problem.

The Prodigy report went on to state:

> When depositors figure this out and accept it emotionally, they will pull cash out of their banks. The fractional reserve banking system is doomed. The Millennium Bug will destroy it in 2000 unless bank runs in 1999 do. I predict the latter. . . . There is no technical solution. There are too many banks around the world. There are too few programmers. Thus you face three options:
>
> (1) The banking system will collapse with *all* of your money in it.
>
> (2) The banking system will collapse with *some* of your money in it.
>
> (3) The banking system will collapse with *none* of your money in it.

Severe food shortages

Such shortages could conceivably be caused by individuals and groups stockpiling essentials in an attempt to minimize the effects of the Millennium Bug. It is very possible that the shocks created and stresses imposed upon the present system by people preparing for the crisis could be more devastating than the Bug itself. The government may deem that intervention is necessary and may put a limit on the stockpiling of necessary items. Preparing for the Y2K problem may be declared "illegal."

Severe social unrest

What happens when crowds of hungry people descend on the stores and there isn't enough to go around? During the gasoline shortage of the late seventies, large numbers of motorists became violent when they were turned away from gas stations.

When the Y2K "crunch" hits, fist fights, brawls, stabbings, and shootings may necessitate the government stepping in and mandating the surrender of all weapons. How will people respond to the order to surrender their weapons? Will we have civilians entering into armed conflict with the military? This condition could be greatly aggravated by blackouts, causing a run on generators, kerosene heaters, and wood burners as the winter of '99 sets in. Prices for fuel may soar at astronomical rates.

What will be the population's response to the imposition of martial law? What will *your* reaction be to curfews, the curtailment of the use of private vehicles, and governmental attempts to relocate citizens for their own "personal safety"? And how will martial law be enforced? Will federal troops fire on locals who do not want to surrender their weapons?

How Will the Constitution Fare?

In the crisis that could erupt out of the Y2K problem, several areas of the U.S. Constitution are in grave jeopardy.

> *Article 1*: Congress shall make no law respecting an establishment of religion, or prohibiting the free exercise thereof; or abridging the freedom of speech or of

the press; or the right of the people to assemble . . .

If martial law is declared, freedom of speech and the right of lawful assembly will have to go.

> *Article 2:* . . . the right of the people to keep and bear arms shall not be infringed.

Will individuals be allowed to protect their food and water from looters and roving bands of thieves? The same weapons that could be used for personal defense could also be used against government troops. Removing everyone's firearms could prove to be disastrous. Many survived the recent riots in Los Angeles because they *had* weapons.

> *Article 10:* The powers not delegated to the United States by the Constitution, nor prohibited by it to the States, are reserved to the States respectively, or to the people.

Under a Y2K-induced crisis, local jurisdictions may have to surrender their authority to "Big Brother." FEMA will send workers into a given area to "help." Is this compatible with Article 10?

The Posse Comitatus Act

If the reports are anywhere near correct, the Y2K problem will create such havoc that it will create a tempting situation to federalize local and state law enforcement agencies.

The *Cato Handbook for Congress,* section 17, "The Expanding Federal Police Power," notes that the use of the military in domestic law enforcement has repeatedly led to disaster. It noted:

> Perhaps the most dangerous effect of over-federalization of criminal law has been militarization of law enforcement. The Posse Comitatus Act of 1878 was passed to outlaw the use of federal troops for civilian law enforcement. The law made it a felony to willfully use "any part of the Army... to execute the laws," except where expressly authorized by the Constitution or by act of Congress.
>
> An army's mission is to rapidly destroy enemies of a different nationality, while law enforcement is supposed to serve and protect fellow Americans, who are guaranteed presumptions of innocence and other rights. The military operates on principles of authoritarian control, with no room for dissent, for waiting for a consensus to form, or for democracy. Military training is antithetical to the values of due process and diversity on which civilian law enforcement must be founded.

Enter the Millennium Bug

Aware of the critical and widespread devastations that the Bug might cause, President Clinton issued Presidential Decision Directive 63 (DD 63). Joseph Farah, editor of *WorldNetDaily.com* and executive director of the Western Journalism Center, an independent group of investigative reporters, stated, in his online "Between the Lines" (June 18, 1998) that DD 63 is "one of the most ominous and least understood orders to emanate from a White

House notorious for issuing such directives. It was released by the White House, like so many others, with little fanfare on May 22." Farah's report went on to quote Senator Robert Bennett, R-Utah, chairman of the Senate Special Committee on the Year 2000 Technology, that a Y2K breakdown will call for martial law. Farah commented by saying:

> The government is getting nervous. To Washington, the Y2K bug threatens to be either the end of centralized control over the lives of Americans or an opportunity to extend the government's power even further.

Though DD 63 does not specifically mention the Y2K problem, it certainly addresses conditions that the problem may cause. In commenting on DD 63 Farah states:

> So what does the White House have in mind? Clinton is calling for a plan to ensure "essential national security missions" as well as general public health and safety by the year 2000. Interesting that he would pick that date. The plan must also provide ways for state and local governments to maintain order. . . .
>
> Not interested in the federal plans? You may have to be. The document states that "it is preferred that participation by owners and operators in a national infrastructure protection system be voluntary." Note that word "preferred."
>
> . . . The military plays a big role in the plans. The Defense Department serves as the "executive agent" through the end of the fiscal year, after which Clinton's

favorite department, Commerce, takes over.

The directive also creates the National Infrastructure Protection Center, which includes the FBI, the Secret Service, other federal law enforcement agencies, the Department of Defense and the intelligence agencies. All federal agencies are ordered to cooperate fully with NIPC. Private businesses involved in critical infrastructure will be "strongly encouraged" to share information with NIPC.

Depending on the nature of the threat, "NIPC may be placed in a direct support role to either DOD (Department of Defense) or the Intelligence Community," the document states.

"Gotcha!"

Through an unbelievable concurrence of carefully orchestrated events, the Y2K trap is about to spring. Through several executive orders, the president now has the power, without congressional approval, to suspend the U.S. Constitution and Bill of Rights. What do these executive orders actually allow the President to do? The following is a partial listing taken from the Internet (see: *http://www.marsweb.com*):

Executive Order 10990: Allows the government to take over all modes of transportation including highways and seaports.

Executive Order 10995: Allows the government to seize and control the communications media.

Executive Order 10997: Allows the government to take over all electric, power, gas, petroleum, fuels, and minerals.

Executive Order 10998: Allows the government to take

over all food resources and farms.

Executive Order 11000: Allows the government to mobilize civilians and work brigades under government supervision.

Executive Order 11002: Designates the Postmaster General to operate a program for the national registration of all Americans.

Executive Order 11003: Allows the government to take over all airports and aircraft, including commercial aircraft.

Executive Order 11004: Allows the Housing and Finance Authority to relocate communities, build new housing with public funds, design areas to be abandoned, and establish new locations for the population.

The words of conservative Howard J. Ruff sum it up quite well:

> ... [The] only thing standing between us and dictatorship is the good character of the President. ...

On the following page is a reproduction of a mandate received by Noah W. Hutchings, president of Southwest Radio Church and one of the authors of this book. A mandate was the highest command in the Roman Empire, coming directly from Caesar. The words clearly circled indicate that unless Southwest Radio Church complies with this dictate, it will have to close its doors. Subsequent information from the IRS indicated that as of 1999 all employers will have to convert to computer transfers of taxes. It would also seem to follow that after 2000 everyone, every taxpayer, will have to obtain an EFTPS number. It should also be noted that this is a NAFTA

> Department of the Treasury   CP 139   JULY, 1996
> Internal Revenue Service
>
> SOUTHWEST RADIO CHURCH OF THE AIR
> 500 BEACON DR
> OKLAHOMA CITY OK 73127-5554
>
> Dear Taxpayer:
>
> **YOU MUST ENROLL AND DEPOSIT ELECTRONICALLY**
>
> Beginning January 1, 1997, you will be required to make your Federal Tax Deposit (FTD) payments by electronic funds transfer (EFT). This requirement is a result of the 1993 North American Free Trade Agreement Implementation Act (NAFTA). NAFTA mandates that businesses making deposits of more than $50,000 in employment taxes for calendar year 1995 make all Federal Tax Deposit (FTD) payments electronically.
>
> The Internal Revenue Code requires you to use the Electronic Federal Tax Payment System (EFTPS) to make your tax deposits electronically. These taxes include those reported on Form 940, Form 941, and Form 943. In addition, you are also required to deposit taxes electronically for Form 720, Form 945, Form 990-C, Form 990-PF, Form 990-T, Form 1042, Form 1120 and Form CT-1.
>
> To use EFTPS, you must first enroll. Since the enrollment process can take up to 10 weeks to complete, we encourage you to enroll now. As of January 1, 1997, you will not be able to deposit these taxes with a check and Form 8109 without incurring a penalty of 10% for the taxes deposited. Delaying your enrollment may prevent you from making your required EFT payment.
>
> We have enclosed an enrollment form for you to complete and send back in the enclosed return envelope. Please read and follow the **Steps to Making Electronic Tax Deposits**. You will receive additional payment instructions after we have completed your enrollment. *PLEASE NOTE: If you are currently depositing taxes electronically through the TAXLINK system you will be required to convert to EFTPS at a later date. We will notify you at the time conversion will take place and you must be enrolled in EFTPS at that time. However, we encourage you to enroll in EFTPS now.*

"mandate." When NAFTA passed Congress, no taxpayer was informed that this foreign or extranational entity would have the authority to collect taxes from United States citizens. Will this authority later be transferred to the World Trade Organization? In view of the Y2K problem, will extranational or international collection of taxes hasten an international computer programming system?

A "Doomsday Hideaway" for Continuity in Government?

Few Americans—and even few congressmen—are aware of a mysterious underground base carved deep inside a mountain near the peaceful town of Bluemont, Virginia, located just forty-six miles from Washington, D.C. Its name: "Mount Weather." Called a "doomsday hideaway" in a 1991 article in *Time* [see from: *http://www.inforamp.net*], Mount Weather is a self-sustaining underground command center for the Federal Emergency Management Agency (FEMA).

It is the backbone of America's "Continuity in Government" program. In the event of a major emergency, the president, his cabinet, and the rest of the executive branch would be "relocated" to Mount Weather. What role will it play when the Millennium Bug makes its appearance?

One could engage in endless speculation, but the facts are that Mount Weather is an underground city that is equipped with a sewage-treatment plant with a ninety-thousand-gallon-a-day capacity, and two tanks holding a quarter of a million gallons of water that could last approximately two hundred people more than a month, plus private apartments and dormitories, cafeterias and hospitals, its own mass transit system, and a television communication system.

six

Being Spiritually Prepared

> Behold, I come quickly: hold that fast which thou hast, that no man take thy crown.
> —Revelation 3:11

Christians are secure in Christ. Whether or not we enjoy victory, however, has much to do with us. This chapter is presented to our readers so that we may be spiritually prepared for whatever the Millennium Bug may throw at us.

The Y2K problem raises issues and questions that strike at the very heart of life as we know it. Not only will the coming crisis possibly rob us of the conveniences that we regard as "essentials," but it may raise moral, ethical, and spiritual questions of unbelievable proportions. Never before has the need been greater that we not be deceived, and never before has it been harder to not stray from the truth. Jesus said: "Take heed that no man deceive you. For many shall come in my name, saying, I am Christ; and shall deceive many" (Matt. 24:4–5). People do not join cults and false religious groups because they want to believe a lie. They join because they are *looking for the truth* and believe that group offers the truth. In other words, *they have been spiritually deceived.*

Success, size, and financial backing of a movement is no indicator that a particular movement or teaching is of God. Gamaliel's words are often cited as a valid measure:

> Refrain from these men, and let them alone: for if this counsel or this work be of men, *it will come to nought*: But if it be of God, ye cannot overthrow it; lest haply ye be found even to fight against God.
> —Acts 5:38–39

This advice is in the Bible, but it is not God's advice to us. Gamaliel was wrong. Does everything that is not of God "come to nought"? If his argumentation were valid, the cults would have died out long ago.

What the Bible Leads Us To Expect
Matthew chapter 13—
Matthew 13 tells us what this age—the period between the first coming of Christ and the Rapture, known as "the Mystery Kingdom" because it was not revealed in the Old Testament—would be like:

1. there will be a sowing of the Word;
2. the Word will meet with a mixed reception—a few will believe, but many will reject it;
3. there will be a parallel sowing of evil;
4. the Kingdom in its mystery form will show tremendous outward growth and apparent success, but on

the inside it will be totally corrupt;
5. this age will end in judgment. It is only then that the righteous and unrighteous will be separated.

The Seven Churches of Revelation—
Bible scholars have long noted the double application of the seven churches. They were real churches, local congregations, in existence during the first century. This is suggested by the local details and reference to specific individuals and situations. But these churches also seem to indicate the progress and condition of the church during the entire Church Age. In other words, they cover the same era of time covered by the parables of Matthew 13.

1. Ephesus—the Apostolic church (A.D. 30–100)
2. Smyrna—the period of Roman persecution (100–313)
3. Pergamum—the age of Constantine (313–600)
4. Thyatira—the Dark Ages (600–1517)
5. Sardis—the Reformation (1517–1648)
6. Philadelphia—the period of missionary expansion (1648–1900)
7. Laodicea—apostasy (1900– ?)

In Scripture "seven" is the number of completion. Laodicea is the seventh and last church. There is no eighth. The church is now poised for the Rapture. The Y2K problem is creating the very conditions prophesied for the end of the age!

More Than a Religion
The Christian faith is more than a religion. It is a rela-

tionship with the resurrected and living Christ. The apostle wrote: "I am crucified with Christ: nevertheless I live; yet not I, but *Christ liveth in me*" (Gal. 2:20). By His Spirit Christ lives in every Christian and is personally present in every Christian's life.

One day an elderly man was walking down a country road. As he looked up he noticed a man vigorously pumping water out of a well. He was amazed at the vigor and persistency of the man. Though he pumped hard he never slowed his pace nor missed a stroke.

As the elderly man drew closer to the well he saw that what he thought to be a man was really a man-sized mannequin. And the mannequin wasn't doing the pumping. The mannequin had been rigged in such a way that the artesian well was doing the pumping! The mannequin was doing nothing but responding to the flow of water.

Christians who are yielded to the Spirit of God can find strength and power to serve the Lord in these desperate times. Christian living is not living with Christ's help. It is Christ *living in us* (Gal. 2:20). Christ doesn't just give us life—He *is* our life. The Scripture says, "When Christ, *who is our life*, shall appear . . ." (Col. 3:4).

We Need Christ—and We Need the Bible

One of the things that cults, false religions, and messianic political movements do is to redefine salvation. Biblical salvation—and that's the only kind worth having—does not come from believing, but from believing in Christ. Faith is nothing. We are not saved by faith in faith. Rather, it is *Christ who saves* through faith. "New Age salvation" comes either from having faith in oneself or in one's ability to have faith. It is a mind game that emphasizes the supposed potential of the human mind to create ultimate reality. It is simply not true that we can achieve whatever we believe. If indeed we could achieve whatever we believe, we wouldn't need a God outside of ourselves. In that scheme, we become our own god.

Similarly, we must also resist the temptation to mysticism. The mystic believes that God communicates directly to an individual's mind apart from Scripture. The mind of the mystic and the mind of God allegedly become one. The mystic confuses his thoughts with God's thoughts and concludes that his thoughts are God's thoughts. Mystics do not believe that they are bound to obey the Bible because they feel authorized to create their own standards of belief and behavior.

This leads those with a mystically-oriented personality to deny the importance of Bible doctrine. Such is often subtly achieved by claiming that truth is more of a feeling than a proposition. This is at the root of much contemporary religious confusion. The Gospel *can* be defined. "I marvel," Paul wrote, "that ye are so soon removed from him that called you into the grace of Christ unto *another* gospel" (Gal. 1:6). "Another" (*heteros*) means "another of a different kind." Truth can be defined. Every "gospel" is not necessarily *the* Gospel.

Just because someone claims to believe in Jesus does not mean that person believes in the Jesus of the Bible. The Jehovah's Witnesses, Mormons, Moonies, and Muslims all claim faith in Jesus. The trouble with doctrinally-inclusive ecumenical groups that say they "believe in Jesus" is that they never specifically define which "Jesus" they are talking about. When a Mormon says, "I believe in Jesus," don't automatically conclude that he is a believer in the Christ of the Bible.

The Ministry of the Local Church
The Body of Christ
Christians need one another. Paul instructed Timothy to not try to "go it alone": ". . . follow righteousness, faith, charity, peace, *with them* that call on the Lord out of a pure heart" (2 Tim. 2:22).

There is a humorous story of a bricklayer who tried to do a job by himself. The following letter makes the point:

> Dear Sir:
>
> I am writing in response to your request for more information concerning Line #10 on the insurance form which asks for "cause of injuries" wherein I put, "Trying to do the job alone." You wrote and said you needed more information, so I am sending you a detailed explanation of my accident.
>
> I am a bricklayer by trade and on the date of injuries I was working alone laying brick around the top of a four-story building when I realized that I had about five hundred pounds of brick left over. Rather than carry the bricks down by hand, I decided to put them into a barrel and lower them by a pulley which was fastened to the top of the building. I secured the end of the rope at ground level and went up to the top of the building and loaded the bricks into the barrel and swung the barrel out with the bricks in it. I then went down and untied the rope, holding it securely to insure the slow descent of the barrel.

As you will note on line #6 of the insurance form, I weigh 145 pounds. But because of my shock at being jerked off the ground so quickly, I lost my presence of mind and forgot to let go of the rope. Between the second and third floors I met the barrel coming down. This accounts for the bruises and lacerations on my upper body.

Regaining my presence of mind, I held tightly to the rope and proceeded rapidly up the side of the building, not stopping until my right hand was jammed in the pulley. This accounts for my broken and mangled thumb.

Despite the sudden pain that shot up my arm, I held tightly to the rope. At approximately the same time, however, the barrel of bricks hit the ground and the bottom fell out of the barrel. Emptied of the weight of the bricks, the barrel then weighed only fifty pounds. I again refer you to line #6 and my weight.

As you would guess, I began a rapid descent. In the vicinity of the second floor I met the barrel coming up. This explains the injuries to my legs and lower body. Slowed only slightly, I continued my descent, landing on the pile of bricks. This accounts for my sprained back and internal injuries.

I am sorry to report, however, that at this point I again lost my presence of mind and let go of the rope and, as you can imagine, the empty barrel crashed down on me. This accounts for my head injuries.

I trust that this answers your question. Please be assured that I am finished trying to do the job alone.

God has given every Christian a "job" to do, and the local church provides the spiritual nourishment, care, and support that will be needed during the Y2K crisis. Larger churches that depend on electricity for lighting, heat, and air will suffer because the Bug may very well turn off the lights and keep them off. Remember, however, that the local church is not a building or a facility. It is a people. In our everyday speech "church" is sometimes used in a misleading way. A news headline stating, "The First Baptist Church Was Totally Destroyed by Fire in an Early Morning Blaze," suggests that the First Baptist Church no longer exists. But though fire may destroy a building, the building is not the church. What, then, is the church? First Corinthians 12:12–27 provides a biblical answer to this important question.

1. The Church is a living organism—
The Scripture compares the church to a body (1 Cor. 12:12, 14 15, 17–18). If the body is to be healthy each part must function in cooperation with the other parts and each part must function in response to the Head.

2. The Church is a Divinely-arranged, gifted organism—
God has arranged the parts of the body just as He wants (1 Cor. 12:18). Believers have been given gifts and placed in the body of Christ in a way that pleases God. The Church is not a haphazard collection of spare body parts.

3. The Church is a caring organism—
Believers will need the nurture of a caring body if the Y2K crisis proves to be as bad as the reports indicate.

First Corinthians 12:25 states: "That the members should

have the same *care* one for another." The word translated "care" conveys the idea of anxiety and concern. As we approach December 31, 1999, there could be a lot of stress. A loving, caring local assembly can make life more bearable. The Bible reminds us that there is a relational aspect to the grace of God, and that this is to be demonstrated through the body of Christ:

> Bear ye one another's burdens, and so fulfil the law of Christ.
> —Galatians 6:2

> And whether one member suffer, all the members suffer with it; or one member be honoured, all the members rejoice with it.
> —1 Corinthians 12:26

> Remember them that are in bonds, as bound with them; and them which suffer adversity, as being yourselves *also in the body*.
> —Hebrews 13:3

The authors of this book believe that the Scriptures teach a pretribulational Rapture of the Church, though there are other scholars who hold to a different scheduling of the Rapture. However, even with our pretribulational position, we do believe that the Church could very well go through some trying times prior to the Tribulation and that the Lord may tarry past the Y2K crisis. Paul Marshall's excellent volume, *Their Blood Cries Out*, documents the worldwide tragedy of modern Christians who are dying for their faith. Christians need to realize that the Lord has provided the fellowship of the Church for a time such as this.

4. The Church is a loving organism—
In a context of teaching on the Church (1 Cor. 12) the apostle brings in God's teaching on *agape* love (1 Cor. 13). There are four points of application that we can make from this:

WE MUST—

▪ *Love One Another*
Since Christians are members of the same body we are to love one another. It would be the height of perversity to hate your own body.

▪ *Help One Another*
Brothers and sisters in Christ are not strangers but family members and should therefore help one another.

▪ *Esteem One Another*
Each part of the body is important. Therefore, we ought to esteem each other (see Phil. 2:3).

▪ *Protect One Another*
The well-being of the entire body is dependent on the health of each member in the body. We must protect one another.

▪ *Worship*
Worship, both private and corporate, is of vital importance to a generation of Christians who are facing the

upheavals that will likely be created by the Y2K crisis. By "private worship" we mean worship that is of the nature of "personal devotions." It includes personal Bible study and prayer and is usually done by an individual in a quiet place. Corporate worship is done publicly in a church building, or public location, set apart for that purpose.

Until a few years ago, most people in America, whether they were believers in Christ or not, regarded Sunday as a day of rest and quiet. A large segment of the population went to church. States and municipalities tacitly encouraged this by mandating that businesses close down on Sunday (Sunday "blue laws"). Several states did not even allow hunting on Sunday.

Today, however, Sunday is no longer given a special place. Sunday is not the Sabbath, and we are not trying to say that it is, but there are an increasing number of activities and opportunities on Sundays that beckon people away from church: sporting events, special sales at malls, easy access via the interstate to lakes, beaches, races, and a whole host of other activities that now compete with church.

With all of the activity on Sunday, fast-food establishments find many hungry patrons. These establishments require their employees to work on Sundays. Christian young people find Sunday to be the day when they can work a full shift, and in this way they too are drawn away from corporate worship.

The Scripture speaks of a time when "the love of many shall wax cold" (Matt. 24:12). We are also seeing this today. Unable to stand against the incessant onslaught of the evil one because they have allowed themselves to be spiritually malnourished, many are unprepared for the spiritual crisis that is to come. The Y2K problem will meet a cold and lethargic Church.

Guarding the Home—
What Moms and Dads Need to Know

Rank humanism is poured into the minds and souls of children, especially from the public schools. Education is not neutral. It is more like indoctrination. More than the "Three Rs" are taught in the classroom. Public education emphasizes:

1. Values Clarification, an allegedly moral neutral approach which is supposed to help children decide their own moral values independently of parental or religious instruction.
2. Development of personal self-esteem. This approach habitually denigrates any approach that speaks of sin or moral failure.
3. The use of various psychotherapeutic techniques which are rooted in an anti-Christian view of man.

Parents need to know that there is a major crisis coming upon the world. The Y2K problem could induce the kind of civil and social chaos that will be very confusing to children. They must be prepared by godly parents.

"As a man thinketh in his heart..."

Our minds are like a computer. What you put in is what comes out. As someone said, "Garbage in, garbage out." God is aware of this and, as our loving heavenly Father, tells us on what to feed our minds:

> Finally, brethren, whatsoever things are true, what-

soever things are honest, whatsoever things are just, whatsoever things are pure, whatsoever things are lovely, whatsoever things are of good report; if there be any virtue, and if there be any praise, *think on these things.*

—Philippians 4:8

Anything that is a matter of spiritual excellence because it is true to the Word of God is what we are to think on. In evaluating our thought life we need to ask the following eight questions set forth in the above verse:

- *Is it true?*

Christians should not dwell on falsehood. Lies destroy people and reputations. They also cause us to misunderstand life.

- *Is it honest?*

The word literally means "honorable." Do you spend time thinking about things that are worthless or have you developed a mental taste for things that are really good?

- *Is it just?*

Something that is "just" is something that is right. It conforms to the principles of equity and justice.

- *Is it pure?*

"Pure" refers to moral purity. That which is impure stains and defiles. This verse rules out pornography.

- *Is it lovely?*

"Lovely" refers to that which is agreeable and pleasant, and leads to peace and harmony.

- *Is it of good report?*

"Good report" comes from a word that means "to speak well of." We need to think on things that speak well of people.

- *Is it excellent?*

This means that we need to think on those things which rise above the ordinary.

- *Is it praiseworthy?*

Does it deserve our praise because it meets with God's approval?

What Kind of Plans Are You Making?

The Y2K problem reminds us that there are going to be a lot of disappointed people in the near future. The *Prophetic Observer* for February 1996 reported on "World Party 2000" and relayed information from a January 10, 1996, Prodigy News Service item:

> Starting to make plans for December 31, 1999? Forget it—you are probably already too late. . . . Although it's still four years off, the changing of the annual odometer to 2000 has already shaped up as the biggest blast of the twentieth century. Guest lists are filled in at some of the world's party hotspots.
>
> The Rainbow Room in Manhattan: there are 470 people ahead of you on the waiting list.
>
> The Savoy Hotel in London: the fortunate can enter a lottery for seats or rooms.
>
> Don't even try the Space Needle in Seattle: it's booked for a private party.

Reservations are piling up for the annual Kaiser ball in Vienna... at the posh La Tour d'Argent restaurant in Paris... at the Waldorf-Astoria in Manhattan.

Looking for something more traditional? Colonial Williamsburg is full and there are 107 names on the waiting list. Good luck visiting Mickey or Minnie. Walt Disney World in Orlando, Florida, reports all seventeen company-owned inns are taken that night.

The list of advanced bookings goes on and on. But, oh, what a night for the Rapture!

These folks have made big plans. Will the Bug cause these plans to come unraveled? It appears that the Bug has his own plans. Make plans for the future, but don't forget the admonition of James 4:13–15:

> Go to now, ye that say, To day or to morrow we will go into such a city, and continue there a year, and buy and sell, and get gain: Whereas ye know not what shall be on the morrow. For what is your life? It is even a vapour, that appeareth for a little time, and then vanisheth away. For that ye ought to say, If the Lord will, we shall live, and do this, or that.

Now Is the Time for Decision!

When people face danger or some imminent crisis, it is natural to do some serious thinking. We may experience regrets that we weren't better spouses, parents, or whatever. Our thoughts may be filled with, "I should have done better." Then comes the promises to God: "If God will only get me through this, I promise to live for Him!"

Recently a man jumped from an airplane and his

chute didn't open. It took him more than a minute to fall three thousand feet. That's enough time for a lot of life to flash before your eyes.

There was another story of a man reported. He woke up in a morgue refrigerator! He had been in a deep coma for twelve hours when he opened his eyes. He cried for help and pounded on the walls of his dark prison. The paramedic who opened the door collapsed and died.

The Y2K problem promises to generate problems of unbelievable proportions. Because our world and society is dependent on computers its effects could very well be devastating.

This impending crisis ought to prod us into spiritual watchfulness. Maybe the Lord will call us to glory before it hits. If not, we need to be spiritually prepared for when it hits.

… seven …

Preparing to Survive

The title of this chapter, "Preparing to Survive," has an ominous tone to it. It paints images of some impending disaster and suggests steps that can be taken to minimize the effects.

The following quotation is taken from the Internet and is listed under "Captain Dave's Survival Center—Y2K: 550 Days and Counting." The author writes:

> In January of 1998, I wrote the following:
> "Captain Dave is no expert, but he believes the physical consequences of the Y2K problem will not be as severe or as permanent as some of the doom sayers are anticipating. But he is still preparing!"
>
> As I revise this document, six months later, I am MUCH more concerned. Nothing I have read or learned reassures me. In fact, I am more worried than ever about the fate of our modern, computer-based civilization.
>
> I was originally planning to weather the storm in our home, figuring we would have some significant disruption of services for a few weeks and then a slow period of shortages, intermittent services, a few riots

in large cities, and then back to normal.

I figured I would be able to band with my neighbors to weather the storm, post a few "looters will be shot" signs, and telecommute or at least stay in touch with my office via the phone.

As I write this, I am planning to spend the days prior and weeks after the turn of the millennium at an isolated retreat in the mountains, heated by wood stove and supplied with water by a spring. While I would prefer—and hope—not to, I am prepared to abandon our home in the suburbs and spend as much of 2000 at this retreat as necessary. I am pre-positioning supplies there, cutting additional firewood, and doing whatever I can to prepare for the worst. I encourage all of you to prepare sooner than later.

Because the closer we get to Y2K, the more expensive and harder it will become to buy everything from a bushel of grain to a gallon of gas.

Some may find this extreme. Others would say that it doesn't go far enough. Complicating the picture and adding a note of gloom are the embedded chips. Embedded chip technologies have enabled us to miniaturize computers so that they can operate in devices with extreme size and weight restrictions. Embedded chips are found in a variety of applications ranging from VCRs and ATMs to kitchen ranges, and oil rigs located on the bottom of some distant ocean. Many of these are date-sensitive and are in hard-to-reach places. It has been estimated that there are some ten million embedded chips in use. Because of their large number and inaccessibility, some argue that it is impossible for programmers to reach them all and make the necessary adjustments.

What Kind of Preparation and How Much?

This is the hardest part of this book to write. How much preparation is really necessary? Do you need food and water for a week? Two weeks? Two years? It would be nice to have enough of everything for as long as is needed, but how much is that? What happens if the stockpiling of food is outlawed?

Some advocate an exodus from the big cities since they are especially vulnerable to Y2K-related problems. Large, populated urban areas have greater potential for devastating food and water shortages, plus problems with utilities and sewer backup. One who lives in a rural area "close to the land" would probably fare much better than someone living in downtown New York City. How can food and other necessities get to a city-dweller when traffic lights, electric power, and mass transit will be out of order? But if large numbers of people move to the country, the country will no longer be the country. Our reaction to the Y2K problem may be worse than the problem itself! If the worst-case scenario develops, will *any* amount of preparation prove sufficient?

A complete and total breakdown will produce effects far beyond our wildest imagination. Perhaps a more likely scenario is a partial breakdown sufficient in scope and devastation to provide globalists with a sufficient excuse to capitalize on the emergency for the sake of promoting their agenda, but not so devastating that no plan will work. There has to be enough left of society for globalists to use the crisis to implement their programs with the willing consent of the population at large.

Our approach is to present the reader with the data and let the reader decide what is necessary to survive. Specific predictions that don't turn out as anticipated discredit the return of Christ. Second Peter 3:3 states "that there shall come in the last days scoffers." Date-setting schemes and unfounded predictions produce scoffers.

There Are Survivalists, and Then There Are Survivalists

If you are making plans to survive the Y2K crisis, are you a "survivalist"?

The word "survivalist" often conjures up images of mean-looking, antiestablishment racists who live in remote regions, and who use Bible prophecy to justify their cache of automatic weapons and explosives. But the term can also refer to anyone who has the will to survive a possible emergency. If you keep a blanket, flashlight, and crackers in your car trunk during the winter months, you have the will to survive.

The Basics of Surviving

If you are convinced that you need to take some steps to help you and your family to survive a Y2K-induced breakdown of society, the following provides some of the basics.

Anticipate Your Most Critical Needs—

This involves food and water and, for those who have special health problems, medication. If you have very young children you will need to make a special effort to see that their needs are met.

Develop a Plan to Meet Those Needs—
A bad plan, or inadequate plan, is better than no plan at all.

Implement That Plan—
Storing food, getting the necessary equipment (generator, water purification system), and learning how to use the equipment is all part of implementing the plan.

Preparing to survive is like insurance. The trick is to know how much you need while operating within your means. Not everyone will agree on how much preparation is necessary. The following illustrates possible levels of preparation.

Level One—
Making preparations for a short-term emergency of minimal effects. Level one will get you through one or two weeks of emergency and is something like preparing for a camping trip. You don't sell your house when you are going camping, nor do you close out your savings account. Level One preparation gives you enough food and water for a week or two and requires a first-aid kit. You plan to go to sleep when it gets dark and get up when it gets light.

Level Two—
This level of preparation is for those who feel the need to make more extensive preparations than those listed under Level One. This level involves securing sources of lighting that will function without electricity—candles, gas lamps—and also storing large quantities of water and food.

Level Three—
This is the most extensive level of preparation. Those who prepare at this level anticipate a long-term crisis of several years' duration that will virtually destroy society as we know it. Water purification systems and generators go along with this level of preparation. Those who seek to attain to a Level Three preparedness will be starting right now and spending several thousand dollars in preparation. Preparation may involve several families pooling their resources and developing their own society complete with their own form of self-government.

What You Can Do—Getting Started

A recent Internet item on *Computerworld* titled "COBOL Pioneer Pitches Year 2000 Fix," reported that Bob Bemer, one of the originators of COBOL and ASCII, has a new product being marketed through his BMR Software, Inc., in Dallas, Texas. The product is called "Vertex 2000." It is supposed to examine a mainframe program's object code and facilitate fixing the Y2K problem. Others, such as Gary North and Leon Kappelman, claim that Vertex 2000 is no "silver bullet" and offers no real hope of averting a Y2K-induced crisis. Most of our readers do not have the technical know-how to evaluate all the pros and cons, but it appears wise to take some precautions and make preparations.

1. For those who have a physical need that requires medication—diabetes, heart irregularities, hypertension—you need either to have a supply on hand or to investigate some alternate sources. The former is a better option, but this should be done in consultation with

your doctor since some medication needs to be stored under special conditions.
2. Start keeping receipts of all bank transactions. Don't trust your bank's computer system to keep this information. In a computer crash it could all be lost.
3. You will need duplicate records of school grades and records for you and your children, tax returns, proof of income, insurance policies, stock certificates, recent statements from investments, birth and marriage certificates, deeds for properties owned, and utility bills. A lot of these things will be of little or no value during the crisis, but they can be very helpful after the crisis in helping you return to a condition of normalcy.
4. Develop a store of food and water.
5. Develop a store of candles, kerosene for lanterns and heaters, flashlights, matches, and firewood.
6. You will need warm clothing, especially in the more northerly areas, since the full force of the Y2K problem will be felt in the winter.
7. You will need portable radios and batteries for their operation in the event that some radio stations are still broadcasting.

You will need to come to a decision about firearms. If you have a store of what others need and want, you will be a target of looters. Many feel that they will need to be prepared to protect themselves in this kind of a situation. Remember, however, that if martial law is declared, firearms may be not be allowed.

The Local Church "Community"
Pastors could encourage their congregations to make

special preparations for the Y2K crisis. The church building could be used for feeding and sheltering those who may need food and water. The church family is a natural community of individuals who can face this crisis together. Church boards need to seriously consider how the resources of the church could be used. Farsighted pastors may be met with ridicule if they suggest the church make preparations to deal with the Y2K problem, but Christians, in times of severe persecution, have pooled their resources. Acts 2:44 says: "And all that believed were together, and had all things common." What are some of the specific things a local church can do?

1. Members should make known their concern about the Y2K problem to the church leadership. Pastors and church leaders are reluctant to tackle a problem that no one perceives to be a problem. But if you voice your concern about the problem they will respond to your concern.
2. Information packets about the Y2K problem need to be prepared so that the membership can become familiar with the issues.
3. At a duly called business meeting the church could constitute a committee to study the problem and make specific recommendations.

A local church can have greater influence on local officials than individuals. Local officials have the power to soften some of the worst effects of the Y2K crisis by making plans to maintain order and prevent widespread violence. Money is not the issue. All that is needed is motivation and foresight.

Who Stands to Gain?

We have no doubt that the Y2K problem is real and that the Millennium Bug will make its appearance. As is true of any complex matter, there are a variety of explanations, assessments, and solutions to the problem. There is a lot of information that is available, but putting it all together and interpreting the data presents a considerable challenge. One thing seems clear, however, and that is that the Y2K crisis will be advantageous to someone.

As we think about the Y2K problem in the light of the Bible's picture of what is coming upon the world, there are four things that must not be forgotten:

1. A one-world religion is but one step away.
2. A one-world government is but one step away.
3. Instant communication is now available for the entire planet.
4. A global economy presently exists.

The coalition of forces that fought in Desert Storm was, it seems to us, more than a coincidence. While the Coalition forces enjoyed victory over Iraq, this victory had a hollow ring for Israel. On January 15, 1995, the *Kansas City Star* carried this report:

> Former Israeli Prime Minister Yitzhak Shamir said he and his cabinet ministers "almost fell off our chairs" when President Bush decided to end the 1991 Persian Gulf War before Iraqi leader Saddam Hussein was toppled. His air force commander described secret Israeli reconnaissance flights over Iraq, clandestine contacts with Jordan's King Hussein and tough bargain-

ing with the Americans, who wanted to keep Israel out of the fighting at any price.

Interesting, isn't It? Israel wanted to eliminate Iraq as a military threat, but foreign powers decided otherwise.

eight

The Final Solution

After reading this book up to this point, you may have a sense of growing foreboding and perhaps even fear. We have shared some things that are both intriguing and frightening. We want this chapter to put it all in proper perspective.

The Importance of Perspective

The story has been told of a young lady who went off to college. It was her first long-term stay away from home. Her parents prayed for her safety and well-being and called her every Friday evening. One day they received a letter from her that went something like this:

> Dear Mom and Dad:
>
> I am writing to inform you of some things that just could not be mentioned on the telephone.
>
> I want you to know that I am recovering from my injuries and doing as well as can be expected. I haven't told you about that because I knew that you would be worried about me. So I waited until seeing some improvement so I could let you know that I am on the mend and will be as good as before in a couple of weeks.

How did I receive the injuries? Well, there was a fire in the girls' dorm. There was a lot of smoke and screaming. The stairway was so filled with smoke that I finally had to jump out of the second story window. Fortunately I landed in some shrubbery and only suffered a few broken ribs and some back injuries. I'm in a lot of pain, but the school doctor says that there has been no permanent damage.

The school moved us into community housing and because of the housing shortage I moved in with this guy. He's really quite a gentleman, but I ought to tell you that his race and religion are different than ours. I am really quite happy, however, and I know that you will understand.

I won't be coming home for the holidays because I get real ill every morning and it makes me feel worse to travel by car.

Gary says "hi." I love you both,

Your daughter

As you would imagine, the young lady's parents were frantic when they received the letter. Her mother had her father call her immediately. When her father got on the telephone, the young lady said: "Well, Dad. None of what I wrote in the letter actually happened. There was no fire. I'm not living with a guy, and I'm not pregnant. But I am getting a 'D' in English and an 'F' in math, and I wanted to help you and Mom put those grades in perspective."

The Bible "tells it like it is," and is absolutely truthful. The Bible tells us the good and the bad. It speaks of the hard times and the good times, but it always puts everything in perspective. It's a perspective fashioned by the grace and mercy of God, and the wonderful truth that, one day, the Lord Jesus Christ will come to remove His church from this world:

> But I would not have you to be ignorant, brethren, concerning them which are asleep, that ye sorrow not, even as others which have no hope. For if we believe that Jesus died and rose again, even so them also which sleep in Jesus will God bring with him. For this we say unto you by the word of the Lord, that we which are alive and remain unto the coming of the Lord shall not prevent them which are asleep. *For the Lord himself shall descend from heaven with a shout, with the voice of the archangel, and with the trump of God: and the dead in Christ shall rise first: Then we which are alive and remain shall be caught up together with them in the clouds, to meet the Lord in the air: and so shall we ever be with the Lord. **Wherefore comfort one another with these words.***
> —1 Thessalonians 4:13–18

They Won't All "Crash"

As we have seen, the Y2K problem may have some devastating consequences because computers everywhere will "crash." But not every computer. In order for the New World Order to be established and the mark of the beast imposed, *someone's* computer will have to work.

Ron Paul's *Legislative Update* for the week of July 13, 1998, revealed the following:

> Just prior to my being elected to Congress, a piece of legislation was passed which was intended to stem

the tide of illegal aliens coming into our country. While the goals were laudable, even the best of legislative intentions can produce results which are reprehensible. Such is the case with an obscure section of the Illegal Immigration Reform and Immigrant Responsibility Acts of 1996. This section authorizes the Federal Department of Transportation to establish national requirements for birth certificates and driver's licenses. The provision... represents an unprecedented power-grab by the federal government and a threat to the liberties of every American, for it would essentially transform state licenses into national ID cards.

... The citizens of states which have driver's licenses that do not conform to the federal standards by October 1, 2000, will find themselves essentially stripped of their ability to participate in life as we know it. On that date Americans will not be able to get a job, open a bank account, apply for Social Security or Medicare, exercise their Second Amendment rights, or even take an airplane flight, unless they can produce a state-issued ID that conforms to the federal specifications.

According to the update no state will technically be forced to accept the federal standards, but the pressure to accept those standards will be there nonetheless. States that refuse to comply will doom their residents because no one would be able to obtain employment, receive Social Security, obtain airline tickets to a destination outside of the state, or have access to medical care.

Representative Paul states:

History shows that when government gains the power

to monitor the actions of the people, it essentially uses that power to impose totalitarian controls on the populace. What would the founders of this country say if they knew the limited government they bequeathed to future generations would have grown to such a size that it claims power to demand all Americans obtain a federally-approved identification card before getting a job?

The good results of legislation are often used as an argument in its favor but, as Paul notes:

> While it is easy to give in to the rhetoric of protecting children or some other defenseless group, we must be cautious that in a rush to provide protection in the short term, we do not do permanent damage to our national heritage of liberty. As Benjamin Franklin once wrote: "Those who would give up essential liberty for temporary security, deserve neither liberty nor security."

If the federal government is going to enforce its standards in this bit of legislation by October 1, 2000, somebody is going to have to kill the Bug in their system. We are rushing toward a crushing global system that will stamp out all opposition. How quickly will it all happen? For a possible answer think of how quickly the Soviet Union fell apart. Think of how quickly we have moved from a society of moral decency to one in which the highest leaders in the land are embroiled in moral scandal *and hardly anyone cares!*

The Final Countdown

As we put things into perspective, where are we now and what is on the horizon?

Judgment on America

Recent earthquakes, floods, droughts, hurricanes, tornadoes, and social unrest are all symptomatic of a nation that has provoked God. Violence in the schools is at an all-time high and is one of the most distressing features of the current scene. The *Dallas Morning News* (July 8, 1998) had a front page story, "Teen Pleads Guilty to Eye-Gouging Attack." The father of the seventeen-year-old high school wrestler said: "He's sorry the boy's injured so badly, but he's not an optometrist. He didn't know how much damage he'd done. It was just a fight. He didn't do it on purpose."

Famines and Pestilences

Our Lord said, "And great earthquakes shall be in divers places, and famines and *pestilences* . . ." (Luke 21:11). One finds it hard to avoid the connection between this Scripture and others like it, with the emergence of multiplied viruses, new strains of bacteria, and immune-system destroying agents. Though modern advances in cancer research and genetic biotechnology have been intended for good, they have given rise to new viruses. Because of the spread of AIDS, and its effect on the immune system, "conquered" diseases like tuberculosis are now showing up in "unconquerable" forms. Los Angeles, San Francisco, and New York are now facing tuberculosis epidemics. Ninety years of tuberculosis control and treatment could now be wiped out (*Los Angeles Time Magazine*, October 24, 1993).

The Increase of Knowledge

No one will deny that there has been an amazing increase in knowledge. Knowledge without parallel moral restraints, however, opens the door to many frightening possibilities. Imagine a monkey holding a machine gun. The monkey knows how to assemble the weapon, load the clip, insert the clip in the weapon, and chamber the first round. But the monkey is vindictive and angry. He has learned that when he presses the trigger coconuts fall off of trees and other monkeys flee.

Cloning technology has put us on the threshold of a "brave new world" and has raised several important questions:

1. Do we believe in the sanctity of human life? Is a human being at the eight-cell stage of division really a human being or merely an aggregate of cells?
2. What is our world view and how does it affect issues such as: abortion, physician-assisted suicide, cloning, and other related issues?
3. Man is to have dominion over the creatures, but what does that mean in terms of our current state of technology? If we have the technical know-how to achieve something, does that mean it ought to be attempted?

Rebuilding the Temple

Several prophetic Scriptures indicate that the Jewish Temple will be rebuilt. Plans for its construction, therefore, are of significance because such plans indicate that the stage is being set for the fulfillment of prophecy.

A major hindrance to the resumption of Temple sacrifices is ritual impurity. In the absence of the red heifer no one can be cleansed from ritual defilement. Under the Mosaic law, priests were purified by being sprinkled with the ashes of the red heifer, as stipulated in Numbers 19. However, since no such ashes are presently available, it is hoped to raise priests from the day of their birth in such a way that they would be kept from defilement. An Internet correspondence from *For Zion's Sake Ministries*, posted March 9, 1998, reported that the *Jerusalem Post* had a recent article titled "First Levites to be Sanctified for Temple Ceremony in 1,928 Years." The article indicated how it is hoped to raise priests from the day of their birth in accordance with strict requirements of ritual purity:

> The idea is to raise a child who from the moment of birth will not touch the dead, not be under the same roof with the dead, and not even be in a hospital, where most babies are born these days, but where the dead are also found.
>
> There is a settlement in the Jerusalem hills which is willing to build a special compound for raising the priestly children.... This will be their living quarters. Between them and the ground—which is also impure, because the dead are buried in it—there will be a partition of air.

Rising Persecution

We do not believe that the Church will go through the Tribulation, but the Church will experience growing persecution. The growing apostasy, governmental antagonism towards the Gospel, politically correct thought, and the breakdown of morality are all factors working together to make believers in Christ look dangerous. Though the door is opening for trade with, and travel to, China, believers are reeling under governmental oppression, and it will get worse, as is indicated by the following report from the *South China Morning Post* (July 10, 1998) Internet edition:

> Guangzhou authorities are preparing to crack down on house church leader Li Dexian to stop his fast-growing congregation getting bigger.
>
> A circular jointly issued by the Guangzhou Public Security Bureau and the municipal United Front Department said Mr. Li had become a formidable influence in Huadu and had repeatedly defied their "education and warnings."
>
> ... Police can send anyone to a labour camp for up to three years for "re-education" without going through the courts.
>
> Guangdong sources said Mr. Li, who lives in Guangzhou, regularly traveled to Huadu to preach. He belonged to the evangelical church.
>
> "Li has been detained and educated many times but his nature is unchanged," the circular said.
>
> ... Religious officials wanted to flex their muscle on house churches after the recent passage of draconian religious regulations by the Guangzhou Municipal People's Congress, the sources said.

A War of Unbelievable Proportions

Zechariah 14:12 states: "And this shall be the plague

wherewith the LORD will smite all the people that have fought against Jerusalem; Their flesh shall consume away while they stand upon their feet...."

Do we possess weapons that produce such an effect? Not only do we possess such weapons, but we've been five minutes away from an accidental nuclear launch aimed at America. The *London Times* for July 13, 1998, reported: "Russian Nukes: Five Minutes to Nuclear War." Russian president Boris Yeltsin had

> activated his "nuclear briefcase" for a retaliatory attack against the West in 1995 when Russian early warning stations picked up what they thought was an approaching American Trident ballistic missile....

The missile turned out to be a Norwegian Black Brent XXII rocket which was part of a Norwegian-American Project investigating the Northern Lights. Bruce Blair, a member of the Brookings Institute in Washington stated: "The military actually issued orders to the Strategic Rocket Forces to prepare to receive the next command which would have been the launch order."

The Final Call

With knowledge comes confidence. In speaking about the future Daniel writes: "... the people that do *know* their God shall be strong" (Dan. 11:32).

Imagine that you are trapped in a burning building. You are on the sixth floor and you dare not open the door to the hallway because the door is hot. So you run to the window and look down to the street. You seem so terribly high. The people and fire engines are so small from where you are. You hear a voice that says, "Jump. We've got a net. We will catch you."

You know you need to get out of the building, but can you trust the voice from below? Is there really a net? You are reluctant to trust the person who told you to jump because you know nothing about him.

But suddenly you hear another voice. "Son, it's Dad. There is a net down here and we will catch you." On the strength of your knowledge of the person down there you jump. Why? Because you know your father. He's no stranger and he has demonstrated his love for you many times over. The *really important* question is this: Is God your heavenly Father?

An Important Question

If you were to walk down Main Street in Anytown, USA, and asked people, "Are you a Christian?" many would answer in the affirmative without really understanding the question.

For some, a Christian is someone who is not Jewish. But that, of course, is not true. In fact, some of the earliest Christians were Jewish.

Others think that a Christian is someone who lives a good life and is a nice person. It's great to live a good life and be a nice person, but that's not what a Christian is. There are many people who are moral, decent, and hardworking, but some will tell you that they are not Christian and don't want to have anything to do with the Christian faith.

Nor does being born in a Christian family make you a Christian. It's wonderful to have Christian parents, but being a Christian is not tied in with genes. A person can be born in a Christian family and not become a Christian. Others have parents who are not Christian and are even opposed to Christianity, but they have become Christian. Christianity is not tied into a certain race, age group, or political persuasion.

Some would like to think that they are Christian because they go to church, but going to church doesn't make you a Christian any more than going to a circus makes you a trapeze artist.

Others trust in baptism and regard it as proof of their Christianity. Some people who have backslid feel it necessary to be baptized again and again . . . but water doesn't save. There is no verse in the Bibe that says water does anything else than make us wet. Country preachers used to say: "You can be baptized so many times that you know every frog in the creek and still not be a Christian."

What, then, is a Christian? A Christian is someone who has trusted Christ alone for salvation. "For by grace are ye saved through faith" (Eph. 2:8). Faith is not doing, but believing. Faith in Christ alone—the kind of faith that saves—is letting go of any hope of getting to Heaven by our own good deeds. "Faith" spells F-A-I-T-H—Forsaking All I Trust Him.

What is your answer to the question: "Why should God let you into Heaven?" If your answer has anything to do with what you have done or are doing, that's a pretty good indicator that you don't understand salvation by grace through faith.

Many answer the above question by saying, "Because I try hard," or, "Because I go to church," or, "Because I'm good to my family." There is nothing wrong with trying hard, going to church, and being good to your family, but none of that impresses God. If you are depending on those things, you are not depending wholly on the finished work of Christ. People who are trusting in their works can never enjoy peace with God. Why? Because they can never be sure that they have done quite enough, or that their works are good enough. Quite frankly, the Bible tells us that our works are not good enough: "All our righteousnesses are as filthy rags" (Isa. 64:6).

Let's go to that burning building again. You decide to jump, and you do. Down, down you go. You land in the net and are safe from the flames. You were saved from certain death. But what saved you? The net, of course. You really were not saved by jumping, because many people have jumped from burning buildings only to be killed in the fall.

Saving faith is like that. Believing does not save any more than jumping saves. Lots of people believe in a variety of people and things, but they are not saved. Just as the net saved you, so it is Christ who saves through faith.

The Final Solution

Some feel that they have made a mess of their lives, and maybe they have. But Jesus Christ came not to call the righteous, but the unrighteous. The publican said, "God be merciful to me a sinner" (Luke 18:13). He was the one made right with God, not the proud, self-righteous Pharisee.

We live in a performance-oriented society. If we perform well in school or on the job, then we will be rewarded with good grades and a job promotion. Most enjoy looking at the Olympics. If an athlete does well that person is overjoyed, but if they perform poorly they are heart broken.

Fortunately becoming a Christian and being saved is not dependent on our performance. Getting to Heaven, *the final solution,* has nothing to do with our performance. It has to do with Christ's performance on our behalf.

How we can rejoice that our eternal destiny is not dependent on the outcome of the Y2K problem!

Important Scritpures to Keep in Your Heart and Mind

And she shall bring forth a son, and thou shalt call his name JESUS: for he shall save his people from their sins.
—Matthew 1:21

For God so loved the world, that he gave his only begotten Son, that whosoever believeth in him should not perish, but have everlasting life.
—John 3:16

He that heareth my word, and believeth on him that sent me, hath everlasting life, and shall not come into condemnation; but is passed from death unto life.
—John 5:24

Not by works of righteousness which we have done, but according to his mercy he saved us, by the washing of regeneration, and renewing of the Holy Ghost.
—Titus 3:5

Now the God of hope fill you with all joy and peace in believing, that ye may abound in hope, through the power of the Holy Ghost.
—Romans 15:13

PART II

===== the transcripts =====

Y2K:
Who? Why? When? Where?

This chapter presents a transcript of five, twenty-five–minute radio programs heard over the Watchman on the Wall program of the Southwest Radio Church, April 27–May 1, 1998. This series was carried over a network of one hundred stations, worldwide by shortwave, and on the Internet.

It is to be understood that when speaking without prepared scripts that verb forms may not agree with subjects, or even that some sentences may be incomplete. Nevertheless, in not wanting to alter sentence structure or edit too closely for fear of changing some meaning by one of the speakers, this transcript is as close to the exact wording as possible:

Monday—April 27, 1998
Dr. N. W. Hutchings and Ken Klein

Hutchings: Many of you are saying, "Well, we don't know anything about the Millennium Bug problem;

we don't want to know anything about it; we don't care anything about it; we think it's a lot of hype." Listen to what the federal government says. I have a memo here in the form of an open letter to the Information Technology Industry, and this is a federal government document as identified at the top.

Today information technology helps federal agencies deliver a wide variety of services that directly affect the health, welfare, and security of every citizen of the United States. Unless government and industry work together, however, some of these information technology systems may not be able to meet their important mission at the turn of the century due to their inability to accommodate the change from the year 1999 to the year 2000. We write to ask you to work with us to solve this critical problem. The government and the information technology industry must work together on this problem to insure the federal agencies acquire only products and systems that are, or will be, 2000 compliant. The coordinated effort is necessary to insure that our citizens receive necessary services upon which they depend. On October 10, 1997, the president signed the Treasury-Postal Appropriation #105-61 which codifies the policy that federal agencies will not buy information technology unless it is the year 2000 compliant."

Here we see the federal government acknowledges that this is a critical problem, and is sending out a plea from Washington to industry in general across the United States to help the government solve this critical problem. Brother Ken, how do you interpret all of this?

Klein: In addition to that, Arthur Gross, who is the chief information officer for the Internal Revenue Service, said this: "Failure to achieve compliance with the year 2000 will jeopardize our way of life on this planet for some time to come." The IRS for the last ten years has been trying to fix their computer system, and they haven't been able to fix it. So, recently, they have put out to private industry that plea for there to be one of the larger corporations in the United States—they've solicited a number of them—to come in and help the IRS solve their Y2K problem, which is the year 2000 problem. They plan on taking the final bid in October of this year, which means they have put out the surrender flag and are trying to get private industry to come in and bail them out. It's hard for me to believe that taking a bid in October 1998 is going to allow for enough time for private industry to come in, working and cooperating with the federal government, to fix the magnitude of the lines of code that have to be fixed in their computers in a matter of time before the year 2000. I don't think they're going to fix the IRS computer system. So, even though they're putting out this plea, it's a little bit late in the day to admit that they're in trouble.

Hutchings: Ken, I have a CNN release here, March 4, 1998, "U.S. Government Gets 'D' for Progress on 2000 Bug," and this is from Washington, D.C., which says, "The chairman of the congressional panel monitoring progress on the so-called Millennium Bug gives the federal government a D-minus Wednesday for its effort to upgrade computer systems for the year 2000." This is a long article about how deficient the government is in getting ready for the year 2000, and how this is going to affect government and industry, and even science, public transportation, and so on. Here's a part that says that cars may not even run.

Klein: Cars have those internal clocks and maintenance systems that are computer connected. Back to the government, there are thirty-five million Social Security checks that are mailed out every month. Social Security, which was hailed as the flagship, the model federal government agency in terms of its working toward compliance, had only completed about eight to ten million lines of code as of the fall of 1997. They had over thirty million lines of code to fix, and they started in 1991, so it took them six years to fix eight to ten million lines of code. Then they found out they had another thirty-three million lines of code, and this is the model agency in the federal government and they're not even a quarter of the way finished in their fixing. Forty-five million people depend on their Social Security checks every month, so the government is in serious trouble. In fact, on February 4, 1998, President Clinton put out executive orders that did not hit the mainstream, and most people don't know about this, but it was called "The Year 2000 Conversion Executive Order." Let me read a paragraph at the beginning of these executive orders. This is what he said:

> The American people expect reliable service from their government and deserve the confidence that critical

government functions dependent on electronic systems will be performed accurately and in a timely manner. Because of a design feature in many electronic systems, a large number of activities in the public and private sector could be at risk beginning in the year 2000. [That is a huge understatement. They are at risk.] Some computer systems, and other electronic devices, will misinterpret the year 00 as 1900, rather than as 2000. Unless appropriate action is taken, this flaw, know as the Y2K problem, can cause systems that support those functions to compute erroneously, or simply not run. Minimizing the Y2K problem will require a major technological and managerial effort, and it is critical that the United States government do its part in addressing this challenge. Accordingly, by the authority vested in me as President by the Constitution and the laws of the United States of America, it is hereby ordered as follows . . .

He then gives his executive orders, and mentions five significant and key areas of concern, and they are banking, telecommunications, public health systems, transportation systems, and electrical power.

The federal government is owning up to the fact that we have a serious problem. It is not something that people should look at and have a glib, complacent, apathetic, and denial attitude about. This is real. It's something that is going to hit us, and I believe that it is extremely prophetic. There is no doubt that the facts are in, and there is enough data coming out every day indicating that we do have a major, major global, worldwide catastrophe looming in the distance.

Hutchings: I have here another interesting article. I get *The European,* and I would just like to read one article.

> Another computer problem: The Euro dollar. Getting computers to recognize dates beyond January 1, 2000, is a big problem, but Europe has one that may be even worse. The European Monetary Union is set to introduce the Eurodollar and all European currency on January 1, 1999, and the computer problems posed by the change seem limitless. There are ATMs all across the continent that will need to be upgraded, and every business will need new software to handle sales, currency, exchange, and taxes. Estimated cost of everything is as high as 400 billion. [Now this is only for Europe.] Worse, the best computer programmers are unavailable because they are busy trying to fix the Year 2000 Bug Problem."

Europe is in desperate need of computer technicians and programmers, but yet they can't get them to convert on January 1, 1999, because the world's best computer technicians and programmers are busy working in the major corporations trying to solve the Millennium Bug. So, in Europe they are in desperate need because they plan on converting the first of next year, and it looks like they might have to wait until January 1, 2000.

Klein: It is really important that we keep our eyes on the rest of the world, as well as what is happening here on the home front, because when you stop to think, for instance, about the banking system, we have a global economic system now. Our banks are connected and tied to the European banking system. Even if we got our banks fixed (which I don't think is going to happen because fifty percent of our banks are only fifty percent completed), only five percent of the European banks have begun. Even if we fixed our own banking system's computers, Europe's would pull us down because we're connected, and their data would re-corrupt our system. So, it's a systemic problem worldwide, and Europe is actually about two years behind the United States, and the United States should have started on this five or six years ago.

Hutchings: Ken, I would like to cite just one example. I think it was in 1982 that the Park State Bank here in Oklahoma that was underwriting the oil industry in Oklahoma and also in nearby states, went suddenly belly up. The reason it went bankrupt all at once was that the Japanese industrialists and bankers, their computers did not work or they chose not to EFT daily deposits to the Intercontinental Bank in Chicago. That started an economic wave that affected branch banks, and the Park State Bank in Oklahoma City, which was one of the most important banks in the southwest, it went belly up. Of course the government rushed in to save Intercontinental Bank—I think it took fourteen billion dollars—but they let poor old Park State Bank here go bankrupt. This is just an indication that when there is a communications problem there is no transfer of funds, satellite problems, and the entire world could be affected financially.

Klein: Speaking of banks, as recently as February 26, in the *USA Today* newspaper (and this was subsequent to Clinton's executive order), Allan Greenspan, who is the Federal Reserve chairman—which is the American banking system's chairman—said this concerning the Millennium Bug problem: "There will be inevitable difficulties which are going to emerge, and you could end up with a very huge problem. [The "could" is an understatement.] The Fed is ready to lend banks tens of billions of dollars if the Bug causes their computers to break down in the year 2000 and they can't make payments." Here we have stepping up—probably more powerful than the president of the United States is Allan Greenspan—ready to throw billions of dollars at the problem in an attempt to fix this. By the way, money isn't the major issue in fixing the Millennium Bug problem. There are two other components to this problem. Number one, there is a fixed point in time that cannot be negotiated, and it's January 1, 2000. You can't change it; it's coming. The other is that there are only a certain number of people—COBOL programmers—that are competent to go back in and fix these lines of code. Even though Greenspan wants to throw money at this, that is not the most important issue. It's the number of people available to fix it and the amount of time we have left. Here we have the banking system shaking, and these government officials stepping up trying to deal with it in the best way they know how to do it.

Hutchings: You have also brought out that some companies, corporations, and systems are already breaking down. I would like to quote from an AP Online article of January 21, 1998, and it brings out: "So Much for the Year 2000 Glitch That Will Gum Up the World's Computers Two Years from Now—The next millennium has already arrived for a growing number of frustrated consumers and businessmen." It goes on to say that AMC Theater offices computer systems will not work now because it won't read the last two numbers. Here's another: "In upstate New York, Corning Incorporated's computer systems for processing supply contracts crashed because the technology couldn't read a couple of zeroes in three year contracts." Here's another system that has crashed because of that also, so it's already beginning to be felt.

Klein: Since the time that Clinton went forward with his executive orders there have been some interesting developments in key leadership in the federal government. Arthur Gross, who was the chief information officer for the IRS, quit; he walked off the job; he just left. Also three key officials from the Department of Defense resigned, and they were over the Y2K problem. So, these things are beginning to drive a lot of our leadership away from their jobs. Maybe they are sensing the futility, and they don't want to have their name on what's a feeble attempt to fix this thing. This is a real problem. My prayers are that people will begin to grasp the magnitude of what's going to be striking us very soon. According to what you're saying, in some of these large corporations they're already having difficulties.

Hutchings: I shared with you an article from *The Euro-*

pean from last fall in October. *The European,* which is the largest international newspaper coming out of Europe, said they investigated the Millennium Bug problem, but this was six months ago. Even so, they said they really didn't see the entire picture. But here are just a few of the things that they verified: The Pentagon has said that some of their missiles may go haywire on January 1, 2000; Gorbachev has warned American senators that the millennium problem could cause serious problems for Russian nuclear power stations. Of course, what would happen if there were two or three dozen Chernobyls in Russia or other parts of the world? Number five, household vessels like cookers and kettles may fail, which would be bad, but if there is no electricity it wouldn't make any difference anyway. Number seven, the year 2000 manager for the British Ministry of Defense likened the scale of the problem to mounting a major combined military exercise continually for the next three years. IBM has told businesses that if they are not working to fix this problem, then it's probably already too late. A British government task force has warned that the millennium problem could lead to riots in the streets. Four airlines have said they will not fly over the millennium to prevent their planes from crashing. Satellites could fail leading to the collapse of international phone links. One of the first to predict a catastrophe in the year 2000 was Arthur C. Clarke, who warned of global chaos. A British minister said pensions won't be paid, and one hundred years of interest could be added to credit card balances. These are just a few of the possibilities that could occur.

Klein: There are so many scenarios that you can play out in so many different ways because just about everything the western world does is dependent upon computer technology. It is so pervasive of a technology that the scenarios are endless.

Hutchings: That is true. We look ahead and see what the Bible says about this. Is such a worldwide catastrophe indicated in the Bible, or the aftermath of such an event? The whole world is operated by computers. Computers are the brains of finance, industry, transportation, and communications, so what happens if a major part of the brain goes dead? Ken, do you see this in the Bible?

Klein: What we have to do as believers is grasp the magnitude of this problem and see it as an opportunity for the ministry of the Gospel. If you're not part of the solution in this matter, you're part of the problem. People need to get on the side of the solution. It is in our best interest to help people know about this. Not only those who are saved, but those who are unsaved, because these are the end times. These are the times spoken of in Scripture. Difficult times will come at the end. Those of us that believe in the Lord really need to take this to heart, look at it, understand it, and then begin to know what to do about it. I've got some steps on what you can do to prepare for the Y2K crisis. First of all, make sure that you're walking right with the Lord. Then, on the practical side of things, protect your financial assets. You need to find alternative sources for water; stockpile a little bit of food; learn to defend yourself; evaluate your present location; purchase adequate clothing; prepare an emergency medical kit; develop an alternative source of heat and energy; find an alternative communications system; steps to safely dispose of waste; and build an emergency preparedness library. Most of all, make sure you're walking with the Lord.

Hutchings: We're not saying that everything we've predicted today is going to happen. We have simply quoted from reliable news sources and credible people who say these things *could* happen. If they could happen, then we should be prepared. We are presenting these programs to inform you so that as a good Watchman on the Wall we sound the trumpet. As these things happen, the guilt, as the Bible indicates, would not be on us, and you would be better informed and better prepared.

◆ ◆ ◆

Tuesday—April 28, 1998
Dr. N. W. Hutchings, Ken Klein, and Dennis Ellenberg

Hutchings: Brother Klein has been on the program several times before, and we're going to be discussing the Millennium Bug. Also, Mr. Dennis Ellenberg is going to be with us. Mr. Ellenberg is a computer consultant for a billion-dollar communications corporation. He's going to be telling us something about the Millennium Bug. Is it really as serious as some are contending it's going to be? I know we have covered this area before, but we're going to be bringing some additional information. Just how will the Millennium Bug—this computer glitch problem—affect the country and all phases of our social, business, and other areas of life in which we live and breathe? Brother Ken, I'll turn things over to you and you can introduce Dennis and continue the discussion.

Klein: Thank you very much, Noah, and I'm very glad to be on with you, and I'm very grateful that you're taking such a vital concern in this important issue, because it will impact every American. In fact, it's a global issue and will touch everyone in the whole world, and it is very prophetic. There are about five main areas that we should be concerned about, and one area that today's guest will speak to. Let me just go over them very quickly. One of them is the electrical power grid (and we'll be dealing with that later), the banking industry, telecommunications, shipping, and health. Dennis Ellenberg works with a large telecommunications company here in the United States, and I'm going let him explain exactly what he does. He is heading up the Y2K program in this large telecommunications company. I'd like to move to him now and have him explain to us exactly what he is involved with at this company. Dennis, if you could tell the audience what you do, and what is your job description.

Ellenberg: First of all, Ken, the program that we have at the company that I'm a consultant for is an enormous program. Like you said before, this is a billion-dollar telecommunications corporation. They're in all kinds of different businesses, and I'm heading up the effort for one of their business units within the overall corporation. Within this organization as a whole they're spending over two hundred million dollars on their year 2000 program. That's over a period of months. They started awhile back and have a very aggressive, a very assertive program, and one of the best in the industry. They're considered an industry leader in what they're doing to prepare the company for the year 2000. What I am doing at this point is gathering inventory of a lot of the suppliers that provide software and products to this company. A company can go in and fix their own internal code problems; they can reprogram and fix it if they have the talent and resources internally to do that. However, if you've gone out and purchased software or a product that is date sensitive from another company, you don't have control over that. You're dependant upon your supplier. That's something that a lot of companies have experienced in today's world of "just in time" manufacturing. I'm sure you've heard a General Motors plant will be shut down because they can't get parts from another plant that was on strike. It's the same way in every business where you're dependant upon suppliers. So the whole logistics of supply-chain management is coming into effect with the year 2000 problem.

Klein: The suppliers of this software, what has been their response to you as you've talked to them about fixing their software? Have they been on the job or . . . ?

Ellenberg: Well, Ken, it's been very frightening in a lot of cases. There's been a lot of information posted on the Internet that's corroborated what I've seen here internally within this company. We had very low response on the number of suppliers that were responding to our surveys. What the company did, they went out and they sent a survey to all their suppliers and said, "You sell services or products to us. We're aware of this problem and we want to make sure that what you're selling us is compliant." In a lot of the contracts they've been putting together, they have year 2000 language in those contracts to insure that if the product doesn't work, and the vendor claims that it does, then it gets into negotiations and lawsuits. Some people are predicting that the litigation from the year 2000 alone will exceed the cost of fixing it. People are estimating on the order of a magnitude of a trillion—with a "T," not a billion—dollars in litigation.

Hutchings: I have a release here from AP dated January 21, 1998, concerning lawyers and the year 2000 computer crisis. This brings out that there are going to be some tremendous lawsuits over this problem, because the companies are not going to have their computer problems fixed. There's going to be a lot of losses incurred. Already, this article says, the United States business companies across the nation are spending 440 billion dollars. What you brought out about lawsuits over the Millennium Bug problem certainly has much credibility.

Klein: What is upper management's attitude as the reality of this is beginning to break upon them?

Ellenberg: One thing that I find interesting is a lot of the way you're putting out information is on the video tape. Telecommunication giant companies employ hundreds of thousands of people, and for those large companies... and I've seen this in more than just the company that I'm working with now... I have seen them actually put together awareness campaigns within their own companies to inform the general population of the issue. So, they have grass roots approaches then, and a lot of times the year 2000 program office will have the ear of certain executive management, and in a company that is so big you are almost dealing with a government-sized agency. There are different levels of concern because people don't perceive the risk. Even internally within companies some subunits of a company will outsource portions of what they do to other areas of the company that have the core competencies. So, internally within companies there's a lot—I don't want to call it bickering or backbiting—but there's a lot of finger pointing on whose responsibility it is to fix this problem. A lot of people in a big company will say, "This is a computer issue. This is a technology issue, so we need to go look at our information technology organization (what used to be termed the data processing group) and they're the ones to fix it," where the people in the awareness organizations are trying to explain to people that this is not really just a technical problem. It is a business problem. It does have a technical solution. It can be fixed. It's not a very hard problem to fix.

The problem is the magnitude of the problem and discovering it, and making sure that you haven't left a rock unturned where you have a critical process that wasn't identified in time.

Hutchings: I have another item here also dated January 21, 1998, and is an AP release, and it contends that the Department of Energy and Labor's computer problem will not be fixed until the year 2019; the Defense Department until the year 2012; Transportation Department until the year 2010; and even in the Social Security Administration there are still thirty million lines of code that have not been fixed. What are we talking about? What is the scope just in the federal government?

Ellenberg: I'll tell you one thing about the statement that it won't be fixed until that stage. To be real honest with you, if your problem in a large government-sized agency or a Fortune 100 company, if you haven't fixed your code by the end of this year, 1998, then you are in deep trouble, because fixing the problem is maybe only half of the effort. The largest portion of the effort in year 2000 remediation of programs to fix the year 2000 bug is testing, because once you go in and fix this code, it all has to be tested to make sure that it operates together with all the other parts. That's the issue that a lot of people are running up against, is they've tightened the schedule so tight that people are saying, "We'll be done December 31, 1999, right before midnight rolls over." If you haven't planned a long period of testing in there, that's really putting you at risk. The scary thing is that the United States government is probably further ahead than the European and Japanese governments. This is a global problem. If you look at it and say, "What is the scope?" it affects all large industries, all governments from the national level down to the local level, anything that has a computer, or things that process electronically that contain dates and time. This affects literally everything that is computer driven.

Hutchings: I heard someone involved in the federal prison system say that he was deeply concerned because not only the federal penal system, but also state, county, and city penal systems are heavily date-oriented. He is concerned about what is going to happen in the prison systems on January 1, 2000. Could that be a matter of concern?

Klein: Like I said, anything that is time and date sensitive information is critical to just about everything that we can think of. But, Dennis, I wanted to ask you a question. We've been talking about your company and its being at the mercy of suppliers of programs to it, and how interconnected this thing is. It's hard for most people to understand how interdependent we are and how much this is a systemic problem, rather than just a problem that is just germane to each individual company. You're over one area in your company. I want to know if telecommunications goes down—and this company is run on information—we're in serious trouble. It is just going to be terrible. What I want to know is, as you investigate your own area, and as you have a general overview of the whole company, tell us, with regard to your company ... and I'm sure you have a feel for the rest of the big companies out there ... what are you finding as you get in there, actually digging into this problem in your own company, what are you discovering about how you're progressing? Are you progressing? Give us a pulse on what you're over and what you think your company's fix rate is so that we can kind of gauge this as we apply it to ourselves. How we can affect long distance services and the flow of information. We need somebody on the inside like you that's dealing with this industry to give us a bird's-eye view of what's happening.

Hutchings: Also, Dennis, would you give us an example, say, if your corporation does not get the problem fixed ... I don't know whether it will or not, but say it doesn't ... how it will affect communications in this country and as related to general business concerns.

Ellenberg: Let me start by giving a really rudimentary explanation of how a phone call is transmitted. When you pick up your receiver on the phone at your home to place a long distance phone call, your phone is being worked by a local phone company. You have phone service with a local regional Bell operating company like Southwestern Bell, even a small independent local exchange carrier, or maybe a big independent like GTE. Once you place that call the local carrier then carries that call to an interexchange carrier which is a long distance company like AT&T or MCI. They pass that call off to the long distance carrier, then that company carries the call to the completing local exchange carrier which could be another regional Bell operating company like Atlanta Bell or Pacific Bell or Ninax, or another company of that nature, and then they complete the call. In that case you have three different companies that are involved in the simple dialing of a long distance phone call. What that means is that these companies have to be able to communicate with each other to pass call-detail records back and forth and to be able to do billing correctly, and to also make sure that the date and times of the calls are all correct. There's a lot of big computing power that is required to do that. It's amazing to me that phone calls are completed as regularly and as promptly and ably as they are, and it's a big credit to the ability of these companies to do business well and to do it cheaply. We have one of the best phone systems in the world here in the United States, but it is all run by computers. If you go to a switchroom for a telephone company, it's full of computers, because that is what a telephone switch is, a computer. So all those computers have to be inventoried, they have to check the software on them, and to make sure that there is no year 2000 problem with them. All those computers that are the telephone switches are made by companies like Nortel, and other companies that are suppliers to the telephone companies, so now you have additional companies involved and it just goes on from there. More and more parts and suppliers into the components that build up the entire infrastructure. That's what the risk is that we're dealing with. There are a lot of different companies that are trying to work together to get this to all come off together. In terms of risk, telecommunications is not just making a phone call that we can call in like we are to this radio show. Telephony is also how we carry a lot of data. A large portion of telecommunications is carrying information across the Internet; information between banks; electronic data interchange; electronic fund transfers for money between banks, companies, and suppliers. So, the telephone network is almost as core to our society and our culture and the way we do business, as is the electrical power grid that allows us to turn on the lights.

Klein: As you begin to dig into all of these things, how are you progressing in what you're over in regard to fixing this problem? Tell us the state of the patient.

Ellenberg: The company that I'm consultant for has one of the most aggressive year 2000 programs that I have seen, and I've seen several from different telecommunications companies, and also non-telecommunication companies. I also work with other consultants that have been in the banking industry, the utilities industry, and the electrical companies. In fact, the person that I met that found this position for me as a consultant was at a year 2000 seminar where Texas utilities was putting on a presentation about how aggressive their year 2000 program is. The people who are making progress, they are solving hopefully the bigger issues. The question is: Are they going to be able to solve enough of the big issues so that things will not grind to a standstill from all of the remaining work that will be left undone when the date rolls around? I think it is very doubtful that any huge corporation, or major government agency, will be one hundred percent completed, because you are dependent upon suppliers over which you have no control. If you want to put a percentage on it, it's really hard to do because internally we can control what code we fix, and we can arrange our schedule, and hire the talent we need to fix the internal systems. It's dependent upon the suppliers. A lot of people are now becoming aware that your supply-chain management is really a make-it-or-break-it issue for being able to survive the year 2000 computer bug.

Klein: So, in your view, as I'm understanding the way you're speaking, we are going to have, maybe not a total collapse in the telecommunications system, but we are going to be severely crippled. Is that a fair analysis?

Ellenberg: Well, Ken, I'd like to be able to say definitely that is what's going to happen, but to be really honest with you, God only knows. The only comfort that I have a lot of times when I get home after a day's work is that God's in control, because I am very fearful of a lot of things that could happen. There are just so many unknowns, so many variables that we really can't know. If you're talking about a local call within a single local exchange or company to your next door neighbor, things like that would not have nearly the risk as calling long distance, and I think that would not be nearly as risky as trying to place international calling.

Hutchings: Is there a possibility that you go to the bank and your bank account might read "zero"; you try to transfer funds, faxes might not work, e-mail might not work?

Ellenberg: I think there are chances for all of that in terms of going to the bank and getting your statement, having a zero balance, or something like that. Most people have hard-copy statements. I get a monthly checking account statement, and I keep those. I would say for someone to be prudent it would be good to keep the last few month's records in order to validate what you had in the account. I think a bigger concern is once the information finally gets out—and that's why I'm so thankful for a radio show like this—is we need to get people this information now so they don't panic at the last minute. That's why I really appreciate Ken's ministry. In fact, I met him when he was coming through Dallas and we've gotten to be friends since then. We need more people to put this information out so that people can be informed; they can take prudent measures now, months in advance, to prepare for this in order so that when the day does get here, if there are problems there won't be mass panic.

Klein: Dennis you've said to us that the company you work for has a very aggressive program, and is one of the company's that is leading the way in Y2K repairs for the telecommunications industry. What about other companies? You must have some sense of the bigger telecommunications companies that maybe aren't as aggressive as yours. Gives us kind of an objective view of the whole industry.

Ellenberg: I hate to name names without actually being on the inside, but I know that some of the long distance carriers that I've worked at in the past have been very slow in getting their year 2000 programs. Let's say AT&T gets every single thing that they needed to get done on their own internal network. Every other long distance carrier that leases lines from AT&T . . . they all have reciprocal agreements in case a piece of fiber cable gets cut by some guy with a backhoe who didn't read the directions "Don't Dig Here," and so they have reciprocal agreements to carry each other's traffic in order to reroute around problems in the network. So they're all dependent upon each other. They may be competitors, but they are also partners in making sure that the whole phone network infrastructure in the country stays up and running.

Hutchings: Dennis, what would you say that might both alert business and management and the average tax payer to this problem in the area of communications?

Ellenberg: If there are any long distance or local telephone company management executives listening, to just encourage them to perceive this as the biggest threat and risk to their business for the next twenty-four months, and to really focus their efforts on making sure they understand the problem comprehensively, and to take whatever measures they can to get their people moving to address it, because the more problems we get fixed now, the less we're going to have to deal with at the last minute.

◆ ◆ ◆

Wednesday—April 29, 1998
Dr. N. W. Hutchings, Ken Klein, and Rick Cowles

Hutchings: We're going to be visiting today, again, with Ken, and also with Mr. Rick Cowles, who is the manager or supervisor of the Y2K program in the utility sector of the Digital Equipment Corporation. We're going to be looking at the Millennium Bug problem as it may affect utilities—general electricity. Anymore, when the electricity goes off it seems like it's the end of the world because you can't communicate. You can't light your office. Everything practically stops. It would be a tragic thing in the world in which we live, that is run by electricity, if all at once there was no electricity. Could that be a possibility? And I'm going to turn the microphone over to Brother Ken Klein, who will be talking to Brother Cowles about this possibility. Yes, or no?

Klein: Thank you, Noah. I want to introduce Rick, and give a little more about his background, so that we can see that he really is a man that we should be listening to. Rick Cowles is one of the leading national experts on the year 2000 computer problem. His extensive analysis of the Y2K issue and the pharmaceutical and electrical utility industry is featured weekly in his column for Westergard 2000, a service of the

Westergard Publishing Corporation. Rick is a frequent guest on national public radio's "The Y2K Investor" program, and is a founding member of the Computer Professionals for Social Responsibilities Y2K Working Group. He's currently serving as the year 2000 program manager of utilities for Digital Equipment Corporation, headquartered out of Digital Equipment's Albany, New York, office.

Rick, thank you so much for joining us today so that we can hear from you about what you know about this problem as it pertains to your areas of expertise. The thing I want to begin with, Rick, was recently you were down in Tampa at the Distributech Conference which bills itself as the world's leading utility information technologies business conference in exhibition. And as I was reading about your take on this thing, I noticed that you came back from that conference very depressed and exhausted. Tell us what happened down there that brought you home with this kind of saddened heart.

Cowles: Well, it was a very eye-opening experience, coming from the standpoint that the businesses that supply equipment to the electric utility industry did not seem to be very tuned into the year 2000 issue. In fact, a lot of the equipment that, in their exhibitions that they were displaying using for sales purposes within the utility industry appeared to have year 2000 issues, and their representatives really couldn't address those year 2000 issues. Just about all the representatives that I spoke with there were either unwilling to talk about it, or perhaps even totally ignorant about the issue.

And when you look at all this equipment that's used in the typical electric utility you've got to wonder if even the utilities themselves are getting the correct information with regards to the year 2000 readiness of this equipment.

Klein: I talk to a lot of people about this problem every day, and most all of them say, "Well, you can fix everything else, but if you don't fix the power grid it doesn't matter what else you fix. If that thing goes down everything else won't work either." The power grid, it seems to me—right there with telecommunications—is the number one issue where we should begin to try to repair this problem. Could you talk to us about the power grid and how it works, so that we can get a better grasp of what it means if this thing breaks?

Cowles: Well, let's take off on your comment about electric power being kind of the cornerstone of industrialized society. And it really is. You mentioned telecommunications. Telecommunications isn't even going to operate properly, or for an extended period of time if there is a problem with the electrical supply. The electric industry in the United States over the last ten or fifteen years has evolved to a very connected industry. Even though you have literally thousands of separate companies that are generating and distributing electricity, they are all tied together in four regional distribution grids (if you want to call them that) within the United States. Those grids receive power and distribute power to and from each one of the individual electric companies. This distribution arrangement that's in place right now was set up in the late 1980s by the Federal Energy Regulatory Commission who foresaw a coming competition in deregulation of the industry and wanted to mandate open access to transmission capacity in the United States. In a real sense also the grids—the individual regional grids—were set up as kind of a fail-safe mechanism for individual utilities. In other words, if a utility has problems within its own system it could draw power off of the regional grid and would in theory make the whole cycle of distribution of power a little bit less fragile than it had been twenty of thirty years ago.

Klein: Now these components work with some kind of relay systems. Is that correct?

Cowles: Each piece of an electric utility business has different issues that need to be dealt with. Let's talk about an individual utility, electric utility, and what makes up that utility. You've got three basic areas. You've got the business end, which is the end that sends out your bill every month. You've got the generation end, which is the part of the business that actually makes the electricity. And then you have the distribution business, which is the wires that run down the street and provide power to homes and businesses. You step back from that for a minute and kind of look at the whole picture and how each one of these business sectors are intertied. And you've got controls in relaying throughout each piece of the business.

Klein: But these relays are all computers.

Cowles: In some cases that's true. In some of the more advanced electric utilities, that is true. In a lot of cases you're dealing with solid state relaying and protected devices that don't necessarily have a computerized input, and that, if anything, may be the saving grace for some portions of the electrical distribution structure, domestically.

Klein: Well, on the ones that the relays that are computers they all have to be looked into, I'm assuming, to make sure that they are compliant with the problems with the Y2K issue.

Cowles: That's correct.

Klein: And are some of these relay systems also embedded chips?

Cowles: Embedded chips is kind of a broad definition of a lot of things within a controlled operation sequence, and at the lowest level a chip itself could have instructions programmed into it to perform a certain action in response to some system condition. How prevalent those are right now it's kind of hard to say because no one has undertaken more than a simple pile of project to look at the extent of this problem and that's where some of the concern within the industry lies.

Klein: So, if you were to give us kind of an analysis at this point concerning the national power grid, let me ask you just a couple of questions about that. In the mainframe computer, where all this converges, how much code do they figure they have to repair?

Cowles: It depends upon the individual utility company, and in particular the size of the utility. A large utility might be running thirty to fifty million lines of code in its business systems that needs to be examined for year 2000 compliance. A smaller utility that doesn't have a terribly extensive customer base, or maybe doesn't have all pieces of the business that I've described before, maybe they are only distributing power and running their business systems. Maybe they are only dealing with a couple million lines of code. So, it's really dependent upon whether someone is getting their electricity from one of the large conglomerates, or whether they are getting it from a small power cooperative.

Klein: How can we access the situation at this point when there are so many variables and components to it? Is it possible to make any kind of assessment over the national power grid's health?

Cowles: I don't know that it's possible to make an overall assessment. As I said before, the national power distribution infrastructure is divided into four separate regions. And the four separate regions are not necessarily dependent upon one another. But again, regionally, all the electric companies are dependent upon each other because of the interconnectedness of the regional power grids and the fact that each electric company has to input their power into, and take their power from, a regional power grid. In terms of assessing one's own readiness of one's own electric company, that's a rather difficult chore because electric companies, like any business, are rather reluctant to discuss their year 2000 programs and what they've analyzed as the potential internal impact, because there's so many legal issues that are involved with the entire year 2000 problem, and certainly electric companies are not immune to that.

In terms of assessing one's own electric company, I think there's a couple things you can do. One is to make an assessment, and there are plenty of resources available to do this, but make an assessment of your own company's exposure by looking at their generation. How much of their power is dependent upon nuclear? Just regional factors, such as climate, can factor into that. And you may also find in contacting your own local utility that they will discuss year 2000 issues and where they are. They are typically not going to tell you what kind of problems they are having, but that's the kind of information that you need to have to make your own personal risk assessment, and kind of plan on what you may do going forward into 1999.

Klein: President Clinton came out with some executive orders. Of course, one of the areas he mentioned, of course, is the electrical industry—the national power grid. Don't they have to make some kind of disclosure to the federal government about their state of affairs? I mean here we are all dependent upon this, yet they won't tell us the facts concerning where it's at, so that we can make the adequate preparations should they stub their toe here.

Cowles: Well, again, one of the problems with the electric utility industry is very similar to most private industries. From a reporting standpoint the only guidance that's in place right now has been put out by the Securities and Exchange Commission who require in financial filing that any investor-owned utility, investor-owned public utility, in its financial filings discuss its year 2000 program, and any material impacts to company operation that may happen as a result of the year 2000.

Hutchings: I have a note here that Gary North says experts say the chance of failure is one hundred percent in the electric grid system. It's going to be a national, international, emergency. Is that not true?

Cowles: Well, Mr. North received that information from me, and actually what I said at the time that I made that assessment was that there was a one hundred percent probability that there were going to be problems within individual regions in the United States—that a large portion of the infrastructure was going to be impacted to one degree or another. I don't think anyone has a crystal ball in front of them that can say what the magnitude or duration of that impact is going to be. But I don't think there's any question that there's going to be some portion of the electric utility industry that is impacted by the year 2000 bug.

Klein: Well, Rick, you said, based upon what I learned at the Distributech '98 Convention, you said, "I'm convinced there is a one hundred percent chance that a major portion of the domestic electrical infrastructure will be lost as a result of the year 2000 computer and embedded systems problem." And then you say the industry is fiddling while the infrastructure burns. What do you mean by the industry is fiddling while the infrastructure burns?

Cowles: What I mean by that is that there are still too many electric companies, and if the largest electric company in the country is prepared for year 2000, but the smallest electric company is not adequately prepared for it, and they're still hooked into the power grid, that big electric company has got as many problems as if their own systems were not prepared because of the interconnectedness of the utilities. And that's where the biggest problem comes in in terms of the companies "getting it." My sense is that there are still too many issues from a legal standpoint that are getting in the way of the industry working on this as a collective effort, rather than individual efforts in each company. And the only way that any of the companies are going to get their hands around this, and understand the impact and the interdependencies, and how these interdependencies impact each other, is to work collectively. And that isn't happening right now.

Klein: Well, let me ask you this question. What should people be doing that are not intrinsically involved in those processes? What could the average person who's listening do in light of what you're saying?

Cowles: I'm not a personal preparedness person. And

my advice on personal preparedness just comes from a personal perspective myself.

I live on the East Coast of the United States. I live in hurricane country. In the basement of my house I have a hurricane preparedness kit that's cycled through on an annual basis. It's got some basic staples, canned food. It's got candles, flashlights, fresh batteries, fresh water. We cycle that through on an annual basis. What I'm saying about personal preparedness is that preparing for power outages, as a result of the year 2000 issue, is not going to be substantially different than preparing for a natural disaster type of scenario where you lose power. The duration could be more.

I'm going to go out on a limb right now, and I'm going to say I don't think it's going to be a situation where everybody in the country is in the dark for a month or two months. I think it's going to be a rotating problem. It's going to be something that's going to be sporadic. That one day you'll have lights and the next day you won't. But in terms of personal preparedness, I think anybody would be well served to have their own disaster preparedness kit in place sitting down in their basement, or up in their attic, or out in their shed, and be able to access that in the event of a problem. I would not recommend that everyone run out and buy a portable generator. And I think the ice storms up in the Canadian provinces bore this out this year, that there were as many problems from people incorrectly using the portable generators that they had at their disposal as there was from the actual lack of power itself.

Hutchings: Rick, there are some things that would be rather inexpensive, like a little camp stove that uses lantern fluid, or how about a little lantern that costs fifteen or twenty dollars. I would think that would be rather inexpensive, and provide light.

Cowles: Kerosene heaters, those are the types of things I would be looking toward. And I think you bring out a good point if you think of it in terms of camping mentality, and if you went up into the mountains for a week, and you took your family camping for a week, what would you need for that period of a week to provide for your family without any outside intervention or involvement.

Hutchings: Every day we get new information about what may happen. I have many, many articles from publications like *The European* warning what could happen. Even here's one from the *Oklahoma Gazette* bringing out what may happen, and it goes on about colliding airplanes, not being able to get money out of the bank, and it says power plants could shut down leaving entire cities in the dark. These are just questions that are being raised about possibilities.

Cowles: Those are all extremely valid questions that need answers, and there's been very little federal leadership. There's been pockets of good state leadership, but there's been very little federal leadership on this issue to look at all of the potential impacts of the year 2000 issue, and to determine whether there are, in fact, valid concerns. I look at it from my own end, from the electric utility industry, and I know that there are valid concerns. Many valid concerns in the electric utility industry.

Hutchings: Well, already we've had brownouts, blackouts, and the backup from one blackout or brownout to another can feed on itself. Is that not true?

Cowles: That's absolutely correct. I think the western power outages that occurred back in 1996 are a very good indicator of the fragility of the distribution network. When a tree limb falling on a distribution wire in Idaho can essentially knock out power to eight states and two Canadian provinces, that's very illustrative of the problems that could happen in a situation where you have one company affecting another company.

Hutchings: Gentlemen, I do appreciate both of you being with us. I know Rick is a manager of the Y2K program of a very large corporation, the Digital Equipment Corporation. He is certainly well informed. He is no novice. I think it would be well for all of us to take his advice and be prepared for a rude awakening on January 1, 2000, or even before. He's given us some very concrete, sensible suggestions, about how we might prepare. Rick, do you have a web site?

Cowles: Yes, I do. Any of your listeners that would like to follow this issue with me can follow it on *www.euy2k.com*.

Hutchings: Thank you, gentlemen, for being with us.

◆ ◆ ◆

Thursday—April 30, 1998
Dr. N. W. Hutchings, Ken Klein, and David Jeffers

Hutchings: On the program today we will be visiting again with Ken Klein of Ken Klein Ministries, the producer of a tremendously informative video, *The Millennium Bug*. Even though we have disseminated several thousand of these videos, Ken has now enlarged the video. He's doubled the length . . . much more information. The Millennium Bug problem just seems to get bigger with each passing day. So, you may want to get a copy of this updated and enlarged video because there is so much new information coming out every day. Also visiting with us today will be Mr. David Jeffers, who is president of Fort Worth Technologies, a computer consulting firm. We're again going to be talking about the Millennium Bug.

What is going to happen January 1, 2000, or even before in the area of computers? You know computers run our lives anymore. They are almost the heart and soul of the industrial economic world. They even influence our daily lives—utilities, banks, checking accounts, whatever. If the computers don't work, or you've got a problem—a glitch—there's going to be a big problem everywhere.

I understand that Mr. Jeffers' consulting firm also writes in COBOL. Ken, you might discuss this further with Brother Jeffers.

Klein: Well, thank you very much, Noah. I'm really looking forward to this interview today, as well as tomorrow. We have David Jeffers from Fort Worth Technologies. David, it's good to be with you again. By the way, ladies and gentlemen, David Jeffers is one of our featured speakers on our *Millennium Bug and Year 2000* video. And he is, as Noah was saying, with Fort Worth Technologies; he's the CEO of that company, and they are very familiar with this problem. They write, rewrite, and modify code every day working with this problem. David, in our video with you, one of the last statements that you make is that the date is not 2000. Many people think the year this is going to crash is 2000, but you say in that statement that we're going to start experiencing problems in 1999. Would you please explain why you made that statement?

Jeffers: Yes, Ken, thanks. It's good to talk to you again, too. Most assuredly we'll be experiencing some problems. One of the more obvious problems that we know is coming up is what we call "packed nines." Now, an open field that you might get from a CD at your bank that's noncompliant, or your driver's license that's noncompliant, the user will typically type in nine at that date because beyond 2000 there's not spaces to go into the twenty-first century. They'll type nines in. That's what we call packing nines. Those nines will come to roost nine, nine, ninety-nine. And those will become active dates at that time. Ninety-nine also has one more problem, Ken. It's an easy keystroke, and it was coded in to be an emergency shut down for mainframe systems. Nine, nine, nine, nine is a fast keystroke to shut a subsystem down. But those are out there like timebombs all over the place, and once nine, nine, ninety-nine comes into fruition, it will simply shut some subsystems down, thinking that it's an emergency shutdown system.

We just recently worked on a system with the city of New York on their licensing department, and that will be coming due July 1, 1999. By the way, when that system was tested out, it did fail.

Klein: You know, one of the things I've been noticing, I don't know if this is the general psychological makeup of the average person in America, but, you know, in the churches today you don't hear much preached about in terms of sin. Hardly anybody talks about hell anymore from the pulpit. In the military you have the "don't ask, don't tell" policy with regard to homosexuality. What is this attitude that you can see in all of that toward objectionable information as it pertains to the IT industry. It just seems like people don't want to admit there's a problem, or face a problem.

Jeffers: Well, I've thought about this a lot because we've been working on this for years, and one of the things that I've discussed with you before is this really gets down to a couple of different issues, the largest being money and security. We have a god in this country, and it is wealth. And when you talk about Fortune 500 companies that I deal with, you're talking about bottom line. You're talking about their stock price on a daily basis, and there is a great amount of disinformation about the potential problem that they have simply to keep stock prices elevated.

Klein: You know we were talking with Rick Cowles about the denial in the industry that he deals with, which is the electrical utility industry, and he's facing the same denial, if you want to call it that, or the aversion to face the truth, with regard to this information. Just as we're seeing with what you're saying, and it's just amazing the general mental state out there of people not wanting to look into this, grapple with it, or even prepare for it. It's just, it's an incredible spiritual issue. That's what I've come to believe about the year 2000 problem. It has to be a delusion that's come over the people with regards to . . . you know Billy Graham, he preached a great sermon on "Your Sin Will Find You Out." And it seems like no matter how much we want to ignore this, every day now it seems like there's something in the papers, somewhere, about the Y2K problem.

Jeffers: Well, denial is not just with the general public. Denial is in my industry, also, and budgets have changed, but they haven't changed radically. The budgets are out for this year; we're not going to do a whole lot more than we did last year. But with a year left we should be testing by '99. That is where people like me are shouting the alarm. I mean, if you want to call me an alarmist, that's fine. An alarmist who knows what I know; a person that you're just going to call an alarmist. I'm just braving out the facts of what's just getting ready to come here. If you're not an alarmist, you're just not seeing the facts for what they are.

Klein: You know, one of the things that we talked about, it seems like six or seven months ago, was what was going to happen to the IT stocks because people would anticipate a company such as yours really spooling up to deal with this problem. Hiring on people and getting contracts to fix government agencies' and private industries' mainframe computers. But that hasn't happened. There hasn't been this big play up in the stock market as it pertains to companies such as yours that would potentially profit from, and richly profit from, dealing with this problem.

Jeffers: It's been a surprise to everyone. Even economists have set up their own companies to invest for year 2000. And some of those places have taken a huge hit because IT stock has not really changed that much.

Klein: So, that even in the investment industry people are not paying attention to this, not believing in it, not wanting to invest in it. Because it seems to me that anybody that is looking at the facts would have to come to the conclusion that, hey, this would be a good investment because of the enormity of the problem, and how much companies have to put into their budgets to fix it. But you're saying the budgets are out, but they're no different than last year.

Jeffers: Not really, not substantially. No.

Klein: And here we are, now pretty well into 1998, and it's still, "stay the course," business as usual.

Jeffers: We're in abject denial, Ken.

Klein: It's unbelievable. We're going to hit the wall with this thing going a hundred and twenty miles an hour, and there's only going to be a few people, a handful of people, so to speak, that are really going to take this to heart, prepare, and get out of harms way as it seems to me.

Jeffers: I agree with you. People are sticking their head above the pack and saying, "Where are we going? We're running off the edge of a cliff here." And the people in my industry know it.

Klein: Southwest Radio Church is one of the only ministries that is really pushing hard on this, and I really appreciate you, Noah, for getting a hold of this, and understanding it, and seeing the prophetic implications. I think, here you are, Noah, in this ministry for sixty-some years, Watchman on the Wall, you're doing your job, and I appreciate you.

I wish other ministries out there would look at this. You know the churches, for example. There's a big conference in Los Angeles with the Four Square people. I sent them my video. They were interested, but, you know, they've got so much to deal with with their ministries, and I'm going, "Don't you understand that you guys probably won't have ministries within about eleven months?" This thing is going to totally dismantle the existing church system because there just won't be money flowing anymore. They won't be able to build their buildings, and fund their programs.

This, this really interrupts and preempts everything that we're doing because it is like a meteorite coming.

In fact, there is a new movie coming out about meteorites, and they're projecting that in thirty years we're going to come very close to a meteor. What would you do if you knew something like that was coming? You would not be doing business as usual. And so this state of denial is, it's remarkable. It reminds me of the time of the Noahic flood when the people were eating and drinking, marrying, giving unto marriage up until the time of the flood. And it seems like that's the stage that we're in today.

Jeffers: Ken, can I interrupt you there with a great quote from the editor of *Computer World*. It's kind of the *Time* or *Newsweek* of my industry, and the editor was pressed pretty hard about why he was not doing more about the year 2000 crisis. And he said, "Show me the meteor. If there was a meteor coming towards earth, show me the meteor. I haven't seen it. Till I see it, I am not going to panic the people out there."

Hutchings: Ken, what we've been talking about the past two days, we've been talking about communications, international communication, satellites, so forth, so on. How the telephone system and communication systems work. Well, if they don't work by the year 2000 we might not even be able to broadcast. Radio stations might have a big problem sending out a signal. Also, we were talking on the last program about the grids. What if there's no electricity. And, of course, we're talking with David today about the problem in general, mainline computers, and correcting this situation—the Millennium Bug.

David, your firm writes in COBOL. I guess you're pretty busy, aren't you?

Jeffers: Oh, we're real busy. We do remuneration of code, which would be either expansion or windowing of COBOL code to bring in the twenty-first century on line on there. But the truth is, there are not enough people to handle the amount that me, and firms like me, have out there.

Klein: David, you know one of the things that's talked about a lot is not just repairing the code—going back in there and putting the two digits back in—but the testing part of it; this parallel testing. The average person doesn't have a clue, and maybe they're not even interested, but testing is a huge part of this. They're saying that fifty percent of the banks are only fifty percent completed, and I'm assuming when they say that, they're talking about just repairing the code. They're not talking about testing that code.

Talk to us about what this means. What has to happen like, say, with a company of like, let's say the IRS, which we know isn't going to make it. They have thirty to sixty million lines of code that we know about that have to be repaired, and they've only, to our knowledge, done about ten million. What do they have to do? And they've had problems that they've caused by trying to repair it. What do they have to do in terms of what has to be done testing wise to a company once they begin to get all their code replaced and repaired?

Jeffers: Well, this is uncharted territory for everybody.

First of all you've got an unpopulated plat that you're trying to test. You cannot move the calendar up to 1999. All you can really do is test your framework that you have. You can't populate that and make changes that day. You can roll the date forward, but that's an unpopulated date. And what happens when you're messing with tens of thousands of millions of lines of code, which is what we're doing, its error begets error again. And while you're in there fixing the date code, you're going to be changing code down and up the line of that binary code which means error begetting error on every line of code. So, it must be tested. Not just to make sure that you're compliant, but to make sure that you catch all the mistakes that you made by going in and messing with every line of code that has a date filled in it. So, if you don't, if you're not testing these systems out, you may have been better off not to even touch the systems.

You're right, places like the IRS are just telling us about their code enumeration. How far along—ten million of sixty million lines of code that they've done so far. When will they get to testing stages? A year ago they were all telling us they were going to give it a year. Everybody's pushed their timeline way forward because we've got a date that's unmovable. It doesn't matter how big you're system is. You're not going to move the date. The date's not, it's irrespective of it, it doesn't care how big your system is. So, everybody who's moving their testing is getting shorter, shorter, and shorter, which, in my opinion, when I've seen this stuff done before, you would have been better off not fixing any of the code in the first place, as to not test it out. By not testing it out you may have doubled the errors that you would have had.

Klein: Well, I've heard that up to three percent of errors are reinjected back into the system after you repair it because of human error.

Jeffers: Minimum.

Klein: And so it has to be tested, retested, and so forth. You're a guy that looks at this problem every day and you have a pretty good grasp of it in so many areas because you deal with different companies and you do your reading and so forth. I think the people listening to you today would be interested in knowing, now that you know all of this, what are you doing personally to prepare for this. I mean, here you are out there with all this sophistication, all this knowledge, trying to fix this. But now as it impacts you, and you see, and you have greater objectivity than the average person, what are you personally doing, David, to prepare for this problem.

Jeffers: Well, first of all I'm not an economist, but I can tell you, from what I know is going to happen, I have done what I feel are some reasonable things. I am out of the stock market. I am going to be liquid cash. I am selling the current house that I have. I'm getting totally debt free. No mortgage. No debt. And I'm moving to a smaller place outside the city. I live in a city, a metroplex, of about five million people, and I'm not going to be living in the city, in the middle of the city, when this deal comes down. I'm going to be moving to either a rural or country area, and that's what me and my wife, and my family, are in the process are doing. We're on our knees. We're seeking the Lord, and this is what He has told us to do. Get out of debt. Get rid of the stock that we have. We're out of our mutual funds because those things are not going to survive a crash like this of the economic system. They're just not. And we're getting ourselves debt free. And that's what we've done. We've sought the Lord. We've done what He's told us to do, so far. And we're waiting for further orders on the deal.

Klein: You know, we were talking the other day, and you were saying, "Ken, I know what it means to sacrifice. And sacrifice does not feel good." You're not doing this because you feel good, or it's comfortable, or it's pleasant.

Jeffers: I have three children under the age of four. And I'm not selling the house that me and my wife have made, and gotten ourselves comfortable for, on some fling. I would not do it, were I not serious. I am. And you're right, I never really knew that sacrifice is doing something that you don't have to do. The Lord pries things out of our hands occasionally, but that's really not sacrifice. Sacrifice is doing something of your own free will, and I know with what the Lord has shown me in the business that I'm in what is coming down the pike. My true desire, and you know this, Ken, is to get out and get the Word to the believers out there, so that they might prepare themselves; so they might minister to those who are going to be in grave need when this happens.

Klein: I really appreciate that because, you know, we are so comfortable with our Americana lifestyle, and we have so much brought into our culture, into Christianity, that we don't really understand what it means to suffer for His sake. We want to know God, and the power of His resurrection, but the fellowship of His suffering, and being conformed to His death side of what it means to be a believer is the part that we just kind of wince from and don't want to embrace. But we're talking here about a problem that God is trying to warn us of in His love. And the average believer is still incredulous, in a state of denial, and not wanting to face this. It's because we are so pampered, and so spoiled, and so pleasure-centered rather than God-centered that many of us are going to be trampled by this. We're not going to be prepared. And we're certainly not going to be able to help anybody else.

That's why we want you to get this video, not just for yourselves, but the key here is to understand that we have a great opportunity to reach America for Christ. We can be a light in the dark. When this hits, people are going to be looking for answers, and we have the answer: Jesus. And this video will help you get the message to your pastors, who are basically so caught up in their churches and their programs that they don't have time to look at this, but it's not going to go away simply because they don't want to believe. And we need everybody's help out there to reach the cities for Christ. This is a tremendous ministry tool.

I think, David and Noah, we are into a time of the greatest harvesting of souls perhaps in the history of the last two thousand years of the Christian era. I just believe that this is a time to be excited. It's not a time to be fearful. Even though we have to make, as you say, David, sacrifices that are not pleasant. They are painful. They are difficult. But we need to be in a position to serve people at the time when they're going to need help the most. And the sooner you can buy into this and believe it and look at the facts and get convicted, or convinced, you're going to be in a position to really be a strength to those who are going to need you in the months ahead.

Hutchings: Thank you, David and Ken. I appreciate you all being with us today. I'm just looking at this story in the *Oklahoma Gazette* by D. Jagger. You're acquainted with him?

Jeffers: Yes, sir. I've spoken with him before. He's one of the top economists in the United States.

Hutchings: He is very concerned about the millennium problem, and he said he'd been screaming it from the housetops since 1983. And he goes on to say, "It's real, I know it's real, and there's a real reason for concern." There are so many articles coming out on the Millennium Bug problem now on the Internet. There's just hundreds of them. The people are gradually becoming concerned about this. But, David, do you think there's a general awakening? Are people pretty much going to remain complacent?

Jeffers: I'm with Ken in one certain aspect, and that is that some people seem so blinded to this. If you have a lot of plans, this is not going to be good for plans. This is not going to be good for a church building program. This is not good if you are building a $500,000 house. This is not good news if you've got a lot of plans.

To a certain extent, I think people's eyes are blinded to this. There's a lot of believers and nonbelievers that I've known, and told, and shared this with, and people I know are simply blinded and refuse to see the truth of this pending deal that's out there.

Hutchings: Well, thank you David for being with us. I'm sure you're going to be busy for the next few months.

Jeffers: I'm going to be busy. I promise you that.

Hutchings: Thanks, Ken. Ken is going to be back with us. We're going to look at this thing from a biblical position. Does the Bible project anything like this that is forecast for the year 2000? We'll have much more to say about the specifics of this problem, and also the prophetic and biblical implications of the Millennium Bug. So, you stay with us.

◆ ◆ ◆

Friday—May 1, 1998
Dr. N. W. Hutchings and Ken Klein

Hutchings: On the program today we are going to conclude a five-program series on the Millennium Bug.

The government has expressed that it is a critical problem. Industry, world finance, and banking are desperately trying to get ready for the year 2000. Even the Common Market and other countries are deeply concerned because they can't even get credible programmers, or computer technicians because they are all working on the larger corporations trying to get ready for the Millennium Bug.

What is the Millennium Bug? Of course, as we brought out, when the mainframe computers were programmed they only used two numbers. They only allowed for two numbers for the date of the year. Like "67" would be for 1967, but now then we come to the year 2000. The computers won't read "00"; they simply go back a hundred years, and that throws everything out of whack. One prison official from the federal bureau, he's even concerned as to what's going to happen in the prisons. Will all the doors swing open? Will the doors shut and not open? Will the records get all fouled up? Who's supposed to leave and who's not? There are so many ways in which this can affect almost every facet of our lives because we are governed, whether we like it or not, by the computer. The traffic lights, the banking systems, whether you cash a check and it's honored or not, whether the lights come on, whether the gas comes on, whether your car runs down the highway even. So, it affects almost every facet of our lives.

We have invented this beast that now holds us in its grasp. And now we read that the beast might go out of whack on the year 2000, and possibly eat us all. It's a very serious problem that is coming upon the world. I'm using these things as analogies, of course, and I'm sure you understand that, as examples. But we believe the Bible may project just something like this; that governments and computer technicians are warning us what may happen in the year 2000. And as we have brought out, it is already happening in some areas.

With me on the program today is Brother Ken Klein. Brother Ken as you look in the Scriptures, what is the possible prophetic scenario from your viewpoint?

Klein: Well, of course, one of the things that I'm finding amazing about this whole issue is how many people I talk to that just don't want to accept it; they don't want to believe in it. Maybe because it's so enormous and such a huge problem they just go into a state of denial. One of the things that the Bible predicts would happen at the end is this. As it was in the days of Noah, so shall it be in the days of the coming of the son of man. People were marrying, eating, and drinking, up until the time of the judgment. In other words, people were living their lives in the routine; in the motions of everyday living; business as usual up until the time that trouble came. And that's what I'm seeing.

I'm seeing that as I talk to people, there's not too many people that want to take this into serious consideration. They just think that somebody's going to come along and fix it. Somehow, it's not to be worried about. It's a little thing. They'll get it handled. And so most people do not look at this very seriously, but the Lord tells us in Scripture that it's going to be at the end just like it was during the times of Noah. And remember there hasn't been a catastrophe of a global nature like this, all encompassing, since the time of the Noahic flood, unless you want to count WWII, but this is going to touch every person on the face of the earth.

So, there has never been anything this big happen since the time of Noah's flood. And that's what it says, "as it was in the days of Noe." So, that's the one thing I'm noticing is the apathy, the denial, the indifference, but for those that are watching, it says that the day will not overtake us like a thief. It will overtake the world like a thief, but not the believers. So, we're watching every day to see the developments of this particular problem coming upon the world, and it's just a remarkable time to be alive.

You know, if you were going to go through the Bible and study the chronologies of people that lived, and nations, and you tracked from the time of Adam to Christ, it was about four thousand years, almost to the year. And from the birth of Christ to now has been two thousand years. In ancient rabbinic tradition there was a prophecy that man would be imprisoned on the earth for six thousand years, and in the seven thousandth year he would be given a rest or release from that incarceration.

Here we are, pressing in on the year 2000 and the greatest technological invention of all time, the computer, is going to end up turning around and biting the human race just at the amount of time that the Bible, at least the rabbis believe, the world would end, so I think it's a very significant time to be alive. Things seem to be wrapping up, and I think there's also a connection here with this Millennium Bug as it pertains to the Middle East, which I would like to get into as well.

Hutchings: Ken, you were talking about the year A.D. 2000. I would like to bring out a scripture here from Hosea, and also about what the early church, even those that sat at the feet of the Apostles taught. Ken, you can pick up where I leave here, leave this subject, or conclude this particular thought. We read in the book of Hosea, and you mentioned the Hebrew tradition about six thousands years. We read in Galatians 4:4 that in the fullness of time God sent forth His Son made of a woman. Fullness of times means there was an exact year, a month, a day, a minute, a second for Jesus Christ to be born in the fullness of time. And I believe it was exactly four thousand years after the creation of Adam. We read here in Hosea 3:4–5: "For the children of Israel shall abide many days without a king, and without a prince, and without a sacrifice, and without an image, and without an ephod, and without teraphim [in other words without a Temple]: Afterward shall the children of Israel return, and seek the LORD their God, and David their king; and shall fear the LORD and his goodness in the latter days."

In the diaspora the children of Israel were scattered all over the world without a Temple. And it says, afterward, after that period is over, they will return. Now we go over to Hosea 5:15: "I will go and return to my place [I think that definitely speaks of Jesus Christ], till they [meaning Israel] acknowledge their offence, and seek my face: in their affliction [or meaning in the Tribulation] they will seek me early." Why are we going to have a Tribulation? It is to prepare Israel mainly to receive their Messiah. Not only to punish the world, and correct the world, and save the world from those who would destroy it, but in this time Israel will turn and believe that Jesus Christ is the Messiah according to Zechariah 12 and Romans 11.

And we continue on: "Come, and let us return unto the LORD: for he hath torn [which God has torn Israel], and he will heal us [that's the promise to Israel]; he hath smitten [Israel for two thousand years], and he will bind us up [which He will]. After two days will he revive us: in the third day he will raise us up [meaning the third millennium], and we shall live in his sight" (Hos. 6:1–2).

Israel has been scattered abroad for two thousand years. One day is with the Lord as a thousand years, as we read in Psalm 90 and 2 Peter 3. And we continue on in Hosea 6: "Then shall we know, if we follow on to know the LORD: his going forth is prepared as the morning; and he shall come unto us as the rain, as the latter and former rain unto the earth" (vs. 3).

During the diaspora the rainfall almost ceased in Israel. It became barren and desolate. When Mark Twain was in Jerusalem in 1867 he said, "This is the most desolate place in the world. Who would ever want to live here?" But now both the former rain and the latter rains have returned in Israel. The rainfall has increased, almost doubled since 1948. So, in the time the latter rains and the former rains will be restored after Israel had returned to the land, after two days, the Messiah would come. That also indicates that we must be nearing the end of this age.

Now I'm not saying that Jesus is going to come in the year 2000, but I say this is very interesting. If you go to the fifteenth chapter of *The Decline and Fall of the Roman Empire*, you will read there that Edward Gibbons in 1770 wrote that those that sat at the feet of the apostles taught that because the heavens and the earth were created in six days that the day of man would be six thousand years, and then would come the sabbath, the millennial sabbath, and Jesus would come back in the year 2000. Gibbons got this information (he was a Catholic) from the archives of the Roman Catholic Church about what the early Christians taught. They actually taught, he said, that Jesus would come back in the year 2000. Now, this was written in 1770. It was by a man who probably was not even a Christian. He was a friend of Voltaire, and he was making fun of what the early church taught. But evidently it was taught.

Again, we are not saying that Jesus could come back in the year 2000, but as you look at everything happening today. You look at the Middle East. You look at what is happening all over the world—the computer system; the increase of crime. We could go on and on—the weather problems; signs in the heavens, and signs in the earth that Jesus referred to; Israel back in the land. What is happening in Israel? It all points to the fact that I don't know anything that has to be fulfilled before the night of the Tribulation falls and then Jesus comes back at the end of the Tribulation. I don't know of any sign yet that has to be fulfilled.

We are not setting dates, because I don't know if

Jesus is coming back in the year 2000 or not, but it is certainly interesting in the light of external evidence, the external signs, and the internal teachings of Scripture.

Klein: You know, another scripture I think is interesting, and it comes into play in Zechariah 12 and 14, when it talks about Jerusalem being a burdensome stone. God could not perform judgment until Israel was back in the land. They started coming back at the turn of the century, but then Israel was made a nation, of course, in 1948.

Now it's the jubilee year in Israel. And one of the more significant things that has happened in the last couple of years is that the U.N. has literally forced Israel to concede land back to the Palestinian Moslems—not only Jericho, but now Hebron, which used to be called Kirjatharba, which was the place where God gave to Abraham the promise, the Abrahamic covenant, that this land would be given to the descendants of Abraham, Isaac, and Jacob forever. And now that they're back in the land the world political body is literally ripping out of the hands of the Jewish people that which God has ordained and covenanted with the Jewish people.

I think that this Millennium Bug problem, it's a global problem, it's coming on all the nations. It very well could be the beginning of God's judgment on the nations for forcing the Lord to enforce that covenant by force. I think it plays right into all the things that are happening at the end time. And it's something to be certainly watched over.

Hutchings: Another interesting thing that I noticed from *The European* is that Europeans have been very conservative in foreign investments and buying of stocks and bonds—that is the monied interest in Europe—because they want to keep the interest money at home. They are building air buses. I did a study on this recently, and in 1929 a lot of stocks and bonds were being held by monied interests in Europe. All at once they started selling stocks and bonds, and that started the selling off of stocks and bonds in the U.S. leading to a run on the banks, and the stock market crash. Now why, all at once, are Europeans buying American stocks and bonds, running the stock market up to almost nine thousand points? Nothing like this has happened since 1929, so it is a warning.

Also, we have here a warning that because of the Millennium Bug something like $440 billion is being spent in the United States on this problem plus $400 billion in Europe. This article here brings out that with all this money being invested in services, or services that are trying to correct the problem, and not into production, that there will be a tremendous drop in stock prices and the whole financial problem is going to have a shock in the year 2000 even if they would fix the bug. That seems to me to be a pretty good barometer—there may be problems ahead.

Klein: Rockefeller in a speech at the U.N. said this: "We are on the verge of a global transformation. All we need is the right major crisis, and the nations will accept the New World Order." Now when you think of that, what do you suppose he was talking about, or what could it possibly be? What global crisis could there be? I always used to think it was a stock market crash or a war, but the Millennium Bug is certainly capable of bringing down the world political and economic system. Now in Revelation 18, starting in verse 9, it talks about the great merchants and the kings of the earth who have committed fornication and lived deliciously with the mystery Babylon. "And the merchants of the earth shall weep and mourn over her; for no man buyeth their merchandise any more" (vs. 11). And then it goes on to say, "And cried when they saw the smoke of her burning, saying, What city is like unto this great city! And they cast dust on their heads, and cried, weeping and wailing, saying, Alas, alas that great city, wherein were made rich all that had ships in the sea by reason of her costliness! for in one hour is she made desolate" (vss. 18–19).

Of course this great city is an analogy of the world economic/political system, Mystery Babylon, that has taken over the whole world. Every city has been infected with this Mystery Babylon. And what could cause in one hour all the great merchants, and all the rich men to weep and mourn? The Millennium Bug. It's going to, in just an hour, when January 1, 2000, hits—nothing is going to work. That could certainly bring down the world economic and political systems, and put us into a vacuum which would necessitate the imposing of a whole new system upon us.

Revelation 13 talks about an end-time system, called the beast system, which will be finalized at the end of time that operates on a mark, called the mark of the beast, and it is the second beast that comes up out of the earth, the false prophet, that sets up the mark of the beast, and it says here that no man may "buy or sell, save he that had the mark, or the name of the beast, or the number of his name." Of course, the Christian community knows and has heard a lot about the mark of the beast, but what could set it up?

Certainly there would have to be tearing down of the existing order for the world to come into a place where nations would accept something as radical as the elimination of our whole money system. Europe is trying to get their new money together, and they're having trouble. They're not going to make it. They have got to deal with the Millennium Bug problem. They don't have time to fix the changeover to their European currency. America is going to have a teetering of her system. Alan Greenspan is trying to throw billions of dollars at it; it's not going to work. What possibly could be the new system?

I believe this is a very prophetic time to be alive, Noah. I believe we are going to see in a short time coming upon the world this beast economic system that has been long prophesied over. It is coming to pass, and it's coming to pass right before our eyes. As we watch daily the events talked about in the newspaper. *BusinessWeek* came out with a cover story on the Millennium Bug. Bill Clinton had his executive orders. Alan Greenspan in the *USA Today*. *Newsweek* talked about it in July of last year—the day the world stops. And every day in newspapers across the country we're hearing more and more about the Millennium Bug. It's all over the Internet. It will be the most important thing that we can talk about this year, aside from President Clinton's troubles, which are just minor compared to what we're all facing.

This system that's coming upon the world will be brought on by the breaking down of the world system as it exists now. Just exactly how David Rockefeller forecast in his speech when he said, once again, "We are on the verge of a global transformation. All we need is the right major crisis, and the nations will accept the New World Order."

Hutchings: We read in Revelation 13:17 of that time, and that no man might buy or sell, save he that had the mark or the name of the beast or the number of his name. And we go on and read the number is 666. We don't try to interpret what the number 666 . . . will it be a computer prefix? We don't know, but Ken let us say that there is a breakdown in the world communications system, satellite system, banking system, economic system, or there are so many problems they can't fix it. Would it be possible that there would be an international computer system brought forward and offered the world so that this problem would never happen again?

Klein: I was in Washington, D.C., and one of my friends that I played college football with is now a three-star general in the Marine Corp. I think he just got promoted to his third star in the last sixty days. I saw him last October, and I said to him, "What are you guys doing about this in the DOD? And he said, "Oh, we're working on it night and day. It's our most serious problem. It even supersedes international terrorism right now." And, of course, you don't read about that in the mainstream newspaper. And I said, "Do you think you're going to make it?" He said, "Well, I think the Marine Corp's computers will probably make it." And I said, "Are you sure?" He said, "No, I'm not sure." And I said, "Well, you guys run contingency scenarios in the bottom of the Pentagon all the time, don't you?" And he goes, "Yeah." And I said, "Well so does the NSA [National Security Agency]. Don't you think they'll come up with something?" And he stopped, and he scratched his head, and he said, "You're right, they probably have figured out some other backup system."

And that's what I think has happened here. We have heard the NSA, which set up the Internet, which Bill Gates is trying to get control over now, as you watch it in the newspapers. He was in Washington, D.C., the last couple weeks fighting in court to see if he could gain control of that. I don't think he will, but I think it's interesting that there's this big struggle now for the gaining of the control of the Internet. The National Security Agency built the Internet, but it seems to me that people that have been running contingency scenarios haven't been asleep at the switch. They've known about this for some time.

Why we haven't had more pressure to fix these systems, globally, over the last twenty years, I don't know. But I do believe that there is a backup system waiting in the wings. I can't say for sure where it's coming from. I have my speculations and guesses. I think it will come out of the United States and England. It'll be the system that will replace the existing system. I think the existing system has got to be scrapped.

There's too much patchwork in it, and we're going to have to start all over. And I think we're going to see it very soon. So, the answer to your question, Noah, is yes. I think there's a system ready to go.

appendix a

Y2K and Signs in the Heavens

In the Olivet Discourse, Jesus indicated with the return of Israel from all nations at the conclusion of the diaspora: "And there shall be signs in the sun, and in the moon, and in the stars; and upon the earth distress of nations, with perplexity; the sea and the waves roaring" (Luke 21:25).

Of course, there are signs in the heavens that as far as we know have never appeared until recent years. These signs are certainly concurrent with the refounding of Israel as a nation and Jews returning from all nations to the land. Radio waves and television waves from one end of the broadcast band to the other, millions of transmissions, are hourly occurring. Where the reader sits there are a variety of radio waves and television waves cascading through his or her body. What harmful effects these radio waves will have on the human body and other forms of animal and plant life in the future remains to be seen. There is serious concern about Extreme Low Frequency (ELF) waves that are now being poured into the atmosphere. The concern here is that

ELF may affect the weather, and as they modulate on the same frequency as the human brain, there may be resulting mental control or damage.

There are also space vehicles and satellites by the hundreds soaring through the heavens, something that was not in evidence until the past forty years. As far as what Jesus meant about signs in the sun and in the moon, we do not need to be in doubt, as these signs are clearly defined for us in other prophetic passages.

Signs in the Sun

1. "... the light of the sun shall be sevenfold, as the light of seven days ..." (Isa. 30:26).
2. "The sun shall be turned into darkness ... before the great and terrible day of the LORD come" (Joel 2:31).
3. "Immediately after the tribulation of those days shall the sun be darkened" (Matt. 24:29).
4. "... the fourth angel poured out his vial upon the sun ... And men were scorched with great heat ..." (Rev. 16:8–9).

Signs in the Moon

1. "... the light of the moon shall be as the light of the sun ..." (Isa. 30:26).
2. "The sun shall be turned into darkness, and the moon into blood ..." (Joel 2:31).
3. "... the sun [shall] be darkened, and the moon shall not give her light ..." (Matt. 24:29).
4. "... there was a great earthquake; and the sun became black as sackcloth of hair, and the moon became as blood" (Rev. 6:12).

In these solar chronology events packed into the very

end of the age, we find three colors: bright, dark, and red. According to the law of thermodynamics:

> As stars are born they must die. Although stars of all types appear to be born in a common way, the collapse and fragmentation, ... the endpoints of a star's life, are highly varied.... [Some] end their lives in the fireworks of tremendous explosions, outshining a galaxy of billions of stars for a short but memorable time.
> —*Origin of Life*, University of Wyoming

Our sun is a medium star. By a process of nuclear fusion (not fission), our star, using its supply of hydrogen, has been doing a good job of providing light and heat for our earth. As hydrogen is converted to helium to iron, etc., the star becomes unstable, with huge dark spots (sunspots) appearing. The dark spots are actually hotter than the bright spots. In its final throes before a nuclear meltdown occurs, the star may become red in color. If the sun becomes dark, the moon will not give any light because the moon reflects only the light of the sun. At a million degrees, a star may become a white dwarf with the shells of the atoms compressed, but not the same gravity of a dark star which may be the result of a trillion-degree nuclear meltdown. In such a compressed star, one teaspoon of star material would weigh one hundred million tons. Not even light could escape from such a dark or neutron star, or black hole.

Stars with a mass eight times the size of our star supernova—in one instant there is a gigantic stellar explosion. Smaller stars nova—there is a semi-explosion with the star becoming hot and bright from seven to fourteen days, ending with star-material being distributed in a circle much like a smoke ring. The small particles, some as large as our moon, will continue to glow and give light, possibly for a thousand years or more. It appears Jesus, John, Joel, and Isaiah clearly predicted a nova of our sun at the time of the Tribulation.

Now what is the association of signs in the sun and moon with Y2K? Increasing sunspots are an evident warning of a nova in a star the size of our sun. Sunspots occur at their peak every eleven and a half years. These cause weather disturbances, communications problems, and even severe damage. The NASA pictures on the next page show the damage caused by a sunspot explosion on March 13, 1989, to a public service transformer. The next sunspot activity is called by NASA "sunspot cycle 23," meaning a huge one. And when will "sunspot cycle 23" reach its highest solar activity? On January 1, 2000 (see picture on page 208).

Now we are not saying that the sun is going to nova on January 1, 2000. However, it does seem more than coincidental. "Sunspot cycle 23" may even complicate the Y2K problem that may confront the world on that date.

PJM Public Service Step Up Transformer—Severe internal damage caused by the space storm of March 13, 1989.

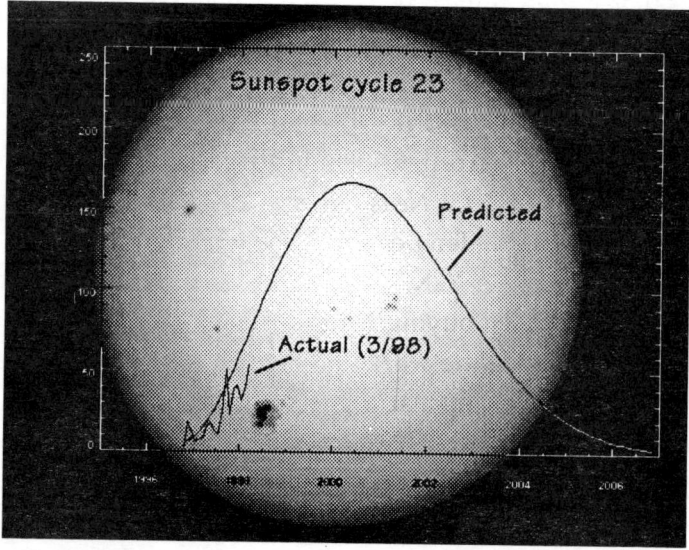

appendix b

Y2K Update

Some choices are hard; others are easy. We have made the choice to not be sensational and to avoid Y2K hype. It is an easy choice. Our goal has been to provide our readers with the facts and to let them decide, under the leadership of the Lord, how they will respond to the year 2000 problem.

Who Is Taking Y2K Seriously?

True or false: It's just the prophecy buffs and hard-core survivalists who are taking Y2K seriously. False. This answer is given in a *New York Times* online report for October 15, 1998: "Ten percent of the nation's executives are stockpiling for Y2K." These executives are stockpiling canned goods, buying generators, and even purchasing handguns. Some were upgrading security on their homes and installing alarm systems that are not dependent on electric power.

Our research shows that agencies all over the U.S. are taking steps to deal with Y2K. Oklahoma governor Frank Keating, as reported in the *Daily Oklahoman* for September 2, 1998, has established a year 2000 task force. Oklahoma hopes to be year 2000 compliant, but in case the state is not, provisions are being made to have National Guard troops on duty. One anticipated problem, however, is voiced by Oklahoma finance director Tom Daxon, who states that "agencies that are not Y2K compliant will have to drop everything to get the job done," but "some agencies are not expected to get legislative funding in time, if at all, to become Y2K compliant."

The city of Denver, Colorado, has made a concerted effort to deal with the year 2000 problem. A listener from Colorado has sent us a letter addressed to all city employees from Denver mayor Wellington E. Webb. The letter, dated October 13, 1998, advises all city employees of an emergency executive order authorizing that they may be temporarily reassigned to other city departments. The executive order also authorizes department managers "to restrict the times and length of annual leave and leave without pay" if deemed necessary as "a curative response requirement" to Y2K. Evidently, lots of people and agencies feel that the problem is real and not imagined. *USA Today* (10/19/98) even had a half-page ad entitled "Are You Y2K OK?" It offered a toll-free phone number (1-800-U-ASK-SBA) and listed more than one hundred and fifty organizations and medium-sized businesses that urge the public to prepare for the year 2000.

The Y2K Threat Still Remains

Since we wrote our book, the experts are still talking about a possible crisis. In fact, the "Millennium Bug" is like other bugs: they seldom travel alone. The *Sunday Oklahoman* for October 25, 1998, had a report entitled "Expert Warns 2000 Bug Not Alone." "If you thought the Year 2000 computer bug was bad, just wait," the report stated. "Other problems that computers may have with dates and data could cost even more to fix and promise to extend well into the next century." The other "bugs" reported:

1. The European Union's conversion to the Euro currency on January 1, 1999;
2. The rollover of the data system in Global Positioning System satellites;
3. The possibility that America could run out of phone numbers, thus requiring the addition of digits to area codes and phone numbers. Adding digits and reprogramming computers is well within the reach of technology. The problem: multiplied thousands of computer programs will have to be adjusted. The time is short, and the cost is high. May a swarm of "bugs" cause an unavoidable Y2K ripple effect?

Y2K and the Already Tottering Economy

Despite rosy media and governmental reports about a strong economy, economists are sounding a less-than-positive note. Robert J. Samuelson, writing for *Newsweek* (10/12/98) states: "The U.S. economy suddenly looks weaker than almost anyone expected. The conventional wisdom still says we won't be pulled down by global economic woes. Don't bet on it." The report, entitled "The Crash of '99?", cites the current economic domino effect that has already made itself felt: first Thailand, then Japan, and then Latin America. At present the stock market and major institutional investors are getting shaky. "The slump in U.S. stock prices reflects a growing recognition that corporate profits will suffer from weaker exports and lower earnings of multinational companies in foreign markets." It's not beyond reason to see that possible power outages, food shortages, the curtailment of travel because radar and other navigational equipment will not function, will inevitably put a wet blanket on an already fizzling economy. Dr. Edward Yardeni, chief economist of Deutsche Morgan Grenfell, "is now predicting a sixty percent chance of a global recession similar in scope to the 1970s oil crisis as a result of Y2K." Yarden has upped his prediction from forty percent to sixty percent because of the minimal progress of the Office of Management and Budgets in dealing with the Y2K problem. Yardeni has concluded that there is an ever-increasing chance that essential government services will be "delayed, disrupted, pared, and curtailed" in 2000.

It May Be Later Than You Think

"The Bug" may hit earlier than originally predicted. January 1, 2000, may be preceded by earlier outbreaks, according to a *CNN Online* report (11/3/98). Hospitals and public assistance programs are particularly vulnerable because "many computer systems that deal with dates often run operations where they need to refer twelve months ahead—meaning that many computers will start to fail on December 31, 1998."

Already, the Y2K "ripple effect" has been evidenced in certain areas. For example, in Honolulu, the electric utility company ran several tests on its power grid to see what would happen. The entire system shut down. In Great Britain computers ordered tons of corned beef destroyed because the computers thought the beef was a hundred years old.

Conflicting Reports—Whom Do You Believe?

Like anything else, there are differences of opinion regarding the extent of the problem. In a recent interview on ABC's "Nightline," John Koskinen, President Clinton's "Y2K doctor," gave a rather optimistic assessment. "I am confident that the vast majority of mission critical systems of the federal government are going to work," he stated. Others, however, have a different assessment. A recent Gartner Group research report continues to give the federal government very low grades on Y2K compliance. As reported on Prodigy (10/27/98), "Health care, education, agriculture, construction, food processing, governments ... are lagging way behind in compliance efforts. Many of these will simply not finish critical systems by 2000." A recent Government Accounting Office study came to a similar conclusion: "The public faces a high risk that critical services provided by the government and the private sector could be severely disrupted by the Year 2000 computing crisis." A House panel report issued in September of 1998 discovered that "more than one-third of the most important [government] systems won't be fixed in time."

Suzanne Peck, who represents the Chief Technology Office of the District of Columbia, as reported on Prodigy (11/3/98), gave a statement in October in which she indicated that Washington, D.C., is a year behind the "recommended timetable." On the same Prodigy report, Senator Moynihan made a chilling statement on Y2K:

> Until now there has been little factual basis on which doomsayers and apocalyptic fear mongers could spread their gospel. After studying the potential im-

pact of Y2K on the telecommunications industry, health care, economy, and other vital sectors of our lives, I would like to warn that we have cause for fear. For the failure to address the millennium bug would be catastropic.

The senator's opening words, "until now there has been little factual basis on which doomsayers and apocalyptic fear mongers could spread their gospel," means that now there really is a solid factual basis for concern.

Big Cities and Small

Y2K is not only an interntional/big city problem. It's a problem that will apparently hit small U.S. cities very hard, according to *USA Today* (10/19/98). Though individual states are spending billions of dollars on being Y2K compliant, many of our nation's 87,259 local governments, including 17,000 police departments and 32,000 fire departments, have not done anything in preparation for the year 2000 problem. In New York State alone, fifty-four percent of towns, forty-eight percent of villages, and twenty-six percent of cities have not even started making plans to deal with "the bug." The report states: "At thousands of city halls and county office buildings across the country, the risks posed by the Year 2000 bug ... are huge. This is where crimes are solved and fires doused, water delivered and sewage disposed of—all with the help of computers."

What About a Manual Override?

Don't computers have a manual override—like automatic cameras allow the photographer to override the meter to get special exposure effects? Some have thought so.

Could this be "the silver bullet" that slays the Y2K bug?

Prodigy (10/29/98) reported, "There's a glitch on watching Mitch," referring to Hurricane Mitch. It had been hoped that a manual override would have gotten the confused GEOS-8 weather satellite that was monitoring Mitch and sending erroneous data straightened out, but it didn't.

> Manual override simply doesn't exist on most systems. In fact, when you hear Y2K debates where people claim that banks, railroads, and power companies can just revert to manual, you know you're hearing words from dreamland. Yes, we did it in 1950, but just as it took decades to get to computer-controlled systems, it would also take decades to go back. For example, if a railroad switch is computer-controlled, and you want to run out to the tracks and flip the lever manually, how exactly do you accomplish that when there is no lever?

Unfortunately, there appears to be "no quick fix for the year 2000 glitch," writes Jon Denton, staff writer for the *Daily Oklahoman* (8/5/98), and that assessment continues to be valid as we move into the winter months of 1999.

What does this mean for the individual? What does it mean for pastors and congregations? Second Peter 3:17–18 is timely:

> Ye, therefore, beloved, seeing ye know these things before, beware lest ye also, being led away with the error of the wicked, fall from your own stedfastness. But grow in grace, and in the knowledge of our Lord and Saviour Jesus Christ.

about the authors

Dr. N. W. Hutchings is president of the Southwest Radio Church, one of the foremost prophetic ministries in the world. He has written dozens of books and booklets on prophecy and other Bible themes. Dr. Hutchings has been active in missions and communications ministries for over 40 years and is recognized for being a world traveler, having led tours to Israel, Iraq, Egypt, Europe, China, and other nations around the world. His plain and conversational style of writing makes the subject matter he approaches both interesting and informative to the reader, regardless of the level of education or understanding.

Dr. Larry Spargimino came from a Catholic background. He became a born-again believer after hearing the gospel of grace through faith. The author changed his eschatological view relating to the Second Coming of Christ from a-millennialism to pre-millennialism while working on his doctorate at Southwestern Baptist Theological Seminary in Fort Worth, Texas. Dr. Spargimino served for several years as pastor of the River Bend Baptist Church in Bristol, Tennessee. He is now an associate pastor and editor with the ministry of Southwest Radio Church.